Donated by
Prolepsis Group
to The Heartland Institute
2015

The CIA and the American Ethic

The CIA and the American Ethic

An Unfinished Debate

Ernest W. Lefever
Roy Godson

Foreword by Ben J. Wattenberg
Afterword by Charles M. Lichenstein

Ethics and Public Policy Center • Georgetown University

Ernest W. Lefever is the founding director of the Ethics and Public Policy Center. He has a B.D. and a Ph.D. in Christian ethics from Yale University. Among the books he has written are *Ethics and United States Foreign Policy* (1957) and *Nuclear Arms in the Third World: U.S. Policy Dilemma* (1979).

Roy Godson is associate professor of government at Georgetown University. He has a Ph.D. from Columbia University. He is the author of several books and articles, most recently *"Eurocommunism": Implications for East and West* (1978).

Charles M. Lichenstein is an independent communications consultant. He is counsel and former senior vice-president of the Public Broadcasting Service.

Ben J. Wattenberg is a senior fellow at the American Enterprise Institute and chairman of the Coalition for a Democratic Majority.

Library of Congress Cataloging in Publication Data
Lefever, Ernest W
   The CIA and the American ethic.
   Bibliography: p.
   Includes index.
   1. United States. Central Intelligence Agency.
I. Godson, Roy, 1942–   joint author. II. Title.
JK468.I6L43   327.1'2'06073   79-6391
ISBN 0-89633-032-X
ISBN 0-89633-031-1 pbk.

$9.50 cloth, $5.00 paper

© 1979 by the Ethics and Public Policy Center of Georgetown University
Printed in the United States of America

Contents

Foreword *by Ben J. Wattenberg*	*vii*
Authors' Note	*ix*
1. Intelligence and the American Ethic Ernest W. Lefever	*1*
2. Congress and Foreign Intelligence Roy Godson	*19*
3. The Role of Pressure Groups Roy Godson	*67*
4. The Performance of TV Evening News Ernest W. Lefever	*96*
Afterword *by Charles M. Lichenstein*	*119*
Appendixes	
A. The National Security Act of 1947	*127*
B. KGB Activities in the United States *Howard Handleman*	*132*
C. Chronology of Intelligence Developments	*140*
Notes	*145*
Bibliography	*153*
Index of Names	*159*

Foreword

BEN J. WATTENBERG

FOR THE BETTER PART of a decade the level of debate about America's intelligence community has been characterized by senators waving dart-guns (under television lights) and denouncing the CIA as a "rogue elephant."

Comes now a slender volume, but long needed: a hard and balanced look at the debate over U.S. foreign intelligence. Professors Ernest W. Lefever and Roy Godson of Georgetown University have asked the right questions, probed the right soft spots. Mr. Lefever's portion of this book focuses on two inquiries: Does gathering clandestine intelligence and engaging in covert action abroad violate the fundamental ethic of a democratic society? Has television been fair in reporting the debate?

Mr. Godson analyzes the complex and sometimes arcane intelligence debate in the Congress. He also profiles the pressure groups seeking to hobble U.S. intelligence and those attempting to make the intelligence establishment strong, effective, and accountable.

This is an important work. It is important for a reason Winston Churchill understood as well as anyone before or since. Churchill understood the tendency of the modern democracies to sow the seeds of their own destruction. In 1955 he anticipated all too vividly what we have witnessed in the past decade. He stated it in the theme of *Triumph and Tragedy,* the sixth volume of his work on the Second World War: "How the Great Democracies Triumphed, and so Were Able to Resume the Follies Which Had so Nearly Cost Them Their Life."

And what are America's follies? We are suffering from a series of self-inflicted wounds that has led to an erosion of our power and influence.

One cause of that erosion is what former secretary of state Henry Kissinger has called the "emasculation of the CIA" through unfair criticism and excessive congressional restraints. Former defense secretary Melvin Laird said the "blunderbuss" congressional hearings "provided a forum for lurid and widely false allegations."

Senator Daniel P. Moynihan characterized the 1977 annual report of the Senate Select Committee on Intelligence as a "profoundly biased political document":

> The committee reports on a world in which very simply, the values which the United States hopefully stands for do not seem to be threatened by any activity save the activities of the U.S. Government, and those of a handful of erstwhile allied or friendly governments. We learn that the intelligence services of the Republic of Korea, the Republic of China, the Philippines, and Iran are possibly threatening the rights of Americans. In fairness, Cuban intelligence services are also mentioned. But nowhere is the Committee for State Security of the Soviet Union (the KGB) even alluded to.
>
> There is a pattern of avoidance of the reality of totalitarian threat throughout this document. This seeming obliviousness to the international context in which our intelligence activities take place seems less an aberration than a mutant of classical isolationism. In my opinion, this may be a comforting world view, but it is a profoundly unrealistic one.

If the Select Committee's view of the world is, as Senator Moynihan states, "profoundly unrealistic," let me assure you that Professors Lefever and Godson are guilty of no such flaw. They are hard-headed scholars—a rare breed. They know that the world is a dangerous place. They believe it would be less dangerous if America once again had a strong, able, self-confident intelligence capability. I believe that, too. And I think the fair-minded reader will believe it after reading this important book.

Authors' Note

THIS BOOK IS BASED on two premises: the survival of Western values and free institutions is gravely threatened from abroad, and to counter these threats the United States must have a vigorous and wise foreign policy informed by effective foreign intelligence services. The scope of our inquiry is limited. We do not attempt to assess the performance of the CIA or any other U.S intelligence agency. We focus rather on the debate over foreign intelligence in a free society. Has this debate in the United States since the mid-1970s reflected a clear understanding of both our national purpose and the dangers and challenges we face? And has there been a candid recognition of the resources and instruments necessary to achieve our national objectives?

In preparing this study we were assisted by a score of scholars and former U.S. policy-makers, some of whom critically reviewed portions of the draft manuscript. We are grateful for their advice. We owe a special debt to Charles M. Lichenstein, whose editorial work through the various stages of the writing was invaluable. He also wrote the afterword, which addresses some of the policy implications of the unfinished intelligence debate. The two authors and Mr. Lichenstein have a similar approach to the issues of foreign intelligence, but each alone is responsible for the writing that appears under his name. A special word of thanks is due Gregory B. Conover, who provided major research support for chapter 4. We also acknowledge the assistance of the TV News Study Center of the George Washington University Library.

Since the debate over the proper role of intelligence is continuing, especially in the Congress, some of our observations about the role of that body may have been overtaken by events. By necessity the inquiry had to be cut off in the spring of 1979. The analysis of the reporting on intelligence by the ABC, CBS, and NBC evening TV news shows covers the period from January 1, 1974, through October 1978.

To give the reader factual background, we have added three appendixes: selections from the text of the National Security Act of 1947, a journalistic account of Soviet KGB activities in the United States, and a chronology of milestones in the intelligence debate. A bibliography is followed by a name index.

ERNEST W. LEFEVER
Professorial Lecturer, International Affairs

ROY GODSON
Associate Professor of Government

November 1979
Georgetown University

The CIA and the American Ethic

CHAPTER ONE

Intelligence and the American Ethic

ERNEST W. LEFEVER

ARE FOREIGN INTELLIGENCE OPERATIONS—clandestine collection, counterintelligence, and covert action, all of which require secrecy and sometimes deception—compatible with the American ethic? Some Americans assert that such activities have no place in a free society. Others insist that they are vital for preserving freedom in a dangerous world. Some support the gathering and analysis of intelligence but oppose covert action designed to influence political developments in other countries. Of all U.S. intelligence operations, covert actions undertaken by the Central Intelligence Agency have been the most controversial, politically and morally.

American leaders have never hesitated to resort to espionage in times of great peril. In 1776 George Washington admonished his generals to "leave no stone unturned" in collecting intelligence against the British, and all our wartime presidents since have taken the same view. But what about intelligence in the twilight zone between peace and war, the condition in which we live today? And what about intelligence as an essentially neutral instrument of foreign policy—as a "reality-defining" resource? Foreign intelligence, in all its variety, is after all simply the art or craft of ascertaining the resources and intentions of other states, friendly and hostile, and in some cases taking covert action to try to change "reality."

A century and a half ago, Alexis de Tocqueville identified the dilemma of diplomacy in an open and democratic society: "Foreign policies demand scarcely any of those qualities which are peculiar to a democracy; they require, on the contrary, the perfect use of almost all those in which it is deficient."[1] A democracy, he said, "cannot combine its measures with secrecy or await their consequences with patience." If this is true of diplomacy it is even more true of intelligence. Americans have always been somewhat uncomfortable with intelligence in peacetime, but since World War II their inhibitions about the use of counterintelligence and covert action have, at least for a time, melted away in the face of a perceived danger from abroad.

Iran: A Microcosm

As a strategically located, oil-rich state, Iran is both an actor in the international drama and a major stage for the larger struggle of power and purpose among the United States, the Soviet Union, and their allies. The turbulent events in Iran in 1978 and 1979—still by no means resolved—reveal the vital role of intelligence as one instrument of foreign policy, along with the military, diplomatic, and economic components. Iran was in a sense a battleground for the foreign intelligence services of Washington and Moscow, albeit one in which U.S. interests may have been ill served, inadequately served, or scarcely served at all.

In November 1978, President Carter said he had been grossly misinformed about the magnitude and significance of the upheaval in Iran; U.S. intelligence had failed him. CIA director Stansfield Turner admitted as much. He argued, however, that the strength of the revolution was a surprise to everyone, that the CIA must "do a better job" in the future, and that he knew of "no other intelligence service that had predicted trouble in Iran."[2]

Former secretary of state Henry Kissinger, for his part, felt that the "emasculation of the CIA" resulting from what he called unfair criticism and excessive constraints in recent years had contributed to the failure of U.S. intelligence in Iran in three ways: (1) it made intelligence analysts overly cautious, (2) it practically deprived us of "covert capabilities," and (3) it altered the balance of expectations within Iran. Elaborating on the last point, he said:

> As late as five years ago opponents of the United States in . . . Iran might well have feared . . . that we simply would not tolerate an assault on the political structure of so close an ally. The various congressional investigations—which incidentally have found very few transgressions—have, however, had the practical result of exhibiting our operating procedures in so much detail that opponents have a precise idea of what we can and cannot do. And congressional restrictions have tied our hands even more. Destroying the mystique of the CIA is in itself a psychological handicap.[3]

Kissinger and other observers said the blame for our failure to anticipate and respond effectively to developments in Iran must be shared throughout the U.S. policy-making system, notably in the State and Defense departments and the White House. But regardless of how the blame is allocated, the United States appears to have lost a staunch ally and gained an oil crisis, and the world now faces the prospect of increased instability in the Middle East and beyond.

U.S. intelligence operations (both collection and covert action) apparently had little effect upon recent developments in Iran. In addition, this country lost vitally important intelligence resources there. In response to reports that leftist guerrillas had wrecked or looted at least two top-secret U.S. electronic listening posts in Iran, Sen. Henry Jackson (D.-Wash.) said this loss "has done irreparable harm for years to come to our capacity to monitor Soviet strategic weapons developments, including some potential Soviet weapons that are constrained by the emerging SALT II treaty."[4] The Ayatollah Khomeini's regime later withdrew permission for the United States to use any intelligence posts in Iran. American officials said, however, that ballistic missile monitoring could be done in Turkey and elsewhere without significantly impairing our capacity to verify Soviet compliance with the treaty.[5] It appears that there will have to be greater reliance on satellites and reconnaissance flights and closer cooperation with British intelligence.[6] Whether or not the SALT II treaty is approved by the Senate, the United States will continue to be dependent on accurate monitoring of Soviet missile testing to gain the necessary information for guiding our strategic arms program.

In contrast, Soviet intelligence in Iran, including covert action, appears to have taken advantage of every opportunity to radicalize the crisis and turn the new rulers against the United States. Soviet activity included incitement to wreck and loot U.S. installations and the discrediting of the American military and economic presence. A report by the Institute for the Study of Conflict (London) stated that the KGB, Moscow's intelligence service, and the GRU, the KGB's military arm, have been active for years in Iran, assisted by huge embassy and consular staffs, 4,600 Soviet-bloc "technicians," and many other "cover" organizations.[7] Iran's armed forces, SAVAK (the Iranian secret police), and workers in the oil installations have been special targets for KGB penetration and recruitment. KGB agents in Iran have sophisticated communications gear and have been trained in sabotage. The KGB, according to the institute, was also responsible for the distribution in Iran of a handsome weekly, *Navid,* that echoed every twist and turn of Moscow's policies. It printed forged documents, and during the summer of 1978 it exploited the Muslim revolt, urging a united front between Islam and Marxism and offering full support of the Tudeh (Communist) party to the anti-Shah struggle. *Navid* spread the rumor that the arson of the Rex Cinema in Abadan, in which hundreds died, was the work of Iranian police.

The KGB also operated a clandestine radio station inside Russia that beamed Persian-language broadcasts to Iran urging the masses to revolt, even as Chairman Brezhnev was warning President Carter not to intervene.[8] The broadcasts called for a national holy war against the Shah and "American imperialism." The radio falsely charged that U.S. officers ordered Iranian troops to fire on demonstrators and that Americans machine-gunned unarmed crowds from helicopters. Some broadcasts issued specific instructions on how to organize riots and make Molotov cocktails.

In October 1978, according to a CIA report,[9] the KGB directed its clandestine agents in the Iranian security forces to take over the leadership of those opposing the Shah as a "stepping stone to second-phase revolutionary activities." Afghan intelligence, now under KGB control, has exploited the presence of some 500,000 Afghan citizens living illegally in Iran. Soviet activity has been aided by the long border—1,400 miles—between Afghanistan and Iran and the deployment of a Farsi-speaking Red Army division on Iran's northern border.

The Four Components of Intelligence

This capsule account of developments in Iran can serve as an introduction to the arcane and morally perplexing world of foreign intelligence and to the special problems it poses for a democratic society. The foreign intelligence service of any state is an instrument of foreign policy that supplements and assists the military, diplomatic, economic, and informational components. Together and separately each instrument is employed to protect the state's security and to advance its external policy objectives. In the broadest sense, intelligence *informs* policymaking.

All the great powers and many of the smaller ones have foreign intelligence services. The larger services perform four major functions: (1) collecting intelligence about other states, (2) analyzing the collected intelligence, (3) engaging in counterintelligence, and (4) conducting covert operations to influence political developments in other states.

Intelligence collection employs many devices and methods, from penetrating foreign governments, obtaining sensitive documents, analyzing the press, and developing contacts with local leaders to engaging in electronic surveillance and satellite photography of military installations. Since much of the desired information can be gathered only by clandestine means in the target country, and most of it only by knowledgeable people, officers and agents must be deployed there on the ground.

Intelligence analysis is based on information from all sources, open and covert, and is carried out by an agency accountable to the head of government. The product of research and analysis takes many forms, including long-range political and economic forecasts for countries or regions, detailed studies of specific problems, resource and intention estimates of particularly influential governments, and analyses of emergency situations that directly involve national interests.

Counterintelligence, vital to any intelligence service, consists of four functions: (1) verifying that collection efforts are bona fide and are not being used by another power to misinform, (2) ensuring that the intelligence services and other government agencies are not being penetrated by the intelligence services of other states, (3) furthering foreign policy objectives by deceiving and misinforming hostile foreign governments, and (4) penetrating intelligence services of other states. In the U.S. system, the CIA is chiefly responsible for counterintelligence abroad and the FBI for counterintelligence within the United States.

Covert operations abroad are designed to alter political, economic, or military realities. They are the most controversial of all intelligence activities because, in addition to secrecy and deception, they sometimes involve lethal force. Covert action includes a wide range of activities, from financially supporting a clandestine radio station, a publication, or a party in a crucial election to providing military or paramilitary aid to certain factions. Covert operations are undertaken to *prevent* developments deemed inimical to the interests of one's nation and to *create* situations in which these interests will be furthered. Such operations often involve intelligence officers and agents whose regular task is to collect information. Some observers believe that covert action should be split off from other intelligence operations—even from the clandestine services—and conducted by a separate organization, but experience suggests that, with proper controls, all foreign intelligence functions can be more effectively performed under one central authority.

Of the four U.S. agencies engaged in foreign intelligence, the

CIA is the best known, partly because of its cloak-and-dagger mystique, partly because it was designed to be the "central" agency within the intelligence community. Two agencies operate under the Defense Department: the Defense Intelligence Agency (DIA), which focuses on the military capabilities and intentions of foreign states, and the National Security Agency (NSA), which is primarily concerned with breaking the codes of other governments and monitoring their communications traffic. The National Reconnaissance Organization (NRO), a joint CIA–Defense Department agency, engages in satellite photography. All four agencies are involved in some secret activities, although the DIA emphasizes "open" intelligence-gathering in accordance with the internationally accepted practice of military attachés of all governments who are assigned to embassies abroad. Satellite reconnaissance is also open, although most of the information gathered remains secret. Washington and Moscow each know the other is photographing its territory.

A distinction should be made among three words commonly used in the intelligence community—secret, clandestine, and covert. *Secret* is the broad, inclusive word, simply referring to activity conducted without the knowledge of others, such as secret meetings or negotiations. *Clandestine* refers to secret activity that is intended to remain secret indefinitely, such as the names of intelligence agents and other sensitive sources of information. *Covert* action is also secret, but it has a public manifestation. For example, if the CIA provides newsprint for an opposition newspaper in a Latin American country, the paper will appear in public, although the public will not know of the CIA involvement. Past CIA support for Radio Liberty and Radio Free Europe is another example.

Intelligence and a Free Society

In our world of continuous conflict, the line between war and peace is often difficult to draw. American interests and values are threatened by the possibility of nuclear war and by the reality of Soviet expansion in the Middle East, Asia, and Africa. The less we know about these and other threats, the more serious they become. Intelligence helps to protect the United States and its allies and to advance our common interests. Like our military preparations, intelligence capabilities and activities are responses to a perceived external threat, or its potential, or to a threatening ambiguity. The threat may be a long-range deterioration of the U.S. position, as in Indochina over the past ten years; a slow-motion crisis, like that in southern Africa; or an immediate and vital challenge to our survival, like Pearl Harbor. Whatever the threat, intelligence has a vital role to play in understanding, deflecting, mitigating, or neutralizing it, or in taking the offensive against it.

As a free and democratic society, a superpower with global responsibilities, and the leader of the free world, the United States is especially vulnerable to the enemies of freedom and self-determination. Most formidable among these is the Soviet Union, whose chief weapon is the KGB, or Committee for State Security, the "sword and shield" of the Soviet Communist party. The KGB employs an estimated half million persons and has responsibilities unprecedented in the annals of state security agencies.

Within the Soviet Union, the KGB acts as the political police, monitoring and enforcing loyalty in all sectors of the society. It spies on diplomats and visiting scholars, businessmen, and tourists. It even has two divisions of elite border troops to prevent the escape of Soviet citizens or the infiltration of hostile agents.

Abroad, the KGB, together with the GRU, its military arm, is the world's largest intelligence service, as well as the most militant, the most pervasive, and the most affluent. The KGB is active in front organizations around the world, in embassies, trade missions, and press offices, in the U.N. Secretariat in New York, and in many other key institutions and agencies within the United States. The KGB is active wherever the Soviet government maintains an ostensibly diplomatic or commercial presence.

The seriousness of KGB activities on American soil was noted by the Senate Intelligence Committee in 1976 and elaborated by FBI director William Webster in a major address in 1978.[10] Soviet agents have ready access to American universities, the press, and a multitude of interest groups, and even to Congress and the executive branch. Webster estimates that there are 1,900 Soviet-bloc operatives in the United States. (Some of the publicly known KGB activities in the United States are noted in Appendix B.)

Monitoring Soviet espionage and covert activity here is essentially an FBI responsibility. This counterintelligence load will become heavier as the number of officials, specialists, and students from the People's Republic of China increases. Our intelligence services have no more urgent task than to comprehend and counter the threat to American freedom and security presented by hostile intelligence services.

The United States is vulnerable abroad because of its long lines of communication to all parts of the world and its multiple responsibilities to distant allies. Even though we have been closing U.S. military bases and have withdrawn tens of thousands of U.S. troops, we still have installations in key places and thousands of military and civilian personnel in more than eighty countries. Overseas Americans, official and unofficial, have been victims of political assassinations, kidnapping, and terrorism.

The Soviet Union is armed with massive nuclear and conventional military power and is supported by growing numbers of strategically located client states in the Middle East, Southeast Asia, and Africa. Its Cuban surrogates are active in Latin America and in more than a dozen African countries. The fall of the Shah has further destabilized the Middle East and exacerbated the global oil crisis. In these circumstances, the United States should have an intelligence capability second to none. We need a great deal more than an effective program of satellite surveillance. We need a capability on the ground for clandestine collection, counterintelligence, and covert action. We need shrewd and well-informed intelligence analysts to help our policy-makers define and interpret foreign realities.

The need for a highly effective foreign intelligence service is a fundamental premise of this study. A second premise is that our foreign intelligence agencies should operate in accordance with the American ethic and the concept of responsible government. They should be accountable to the President, and their activities and financing should be subject to congressional oversight. Because we are a democracy, our foreign intelligence activities should in the broadest sense be understood and supported by the American people. The media of mass communications should present a fair and balanced picture of the rationale for and the activities of U.S. intelligence, including, of course, responsible criticism of flaws, weaknesses, and abuses.

Virtually all informed observers acknowledge that America's foreign intelligence capability has been weakened rather than strengthened over the past five or so years, primarily by sensational criticism in the press and excessive congressional constraints. Former defense secretary Melvin R. Laird takes the same position as Henry Kissinger, cited earlier. "Since 1974," Laird said, "the CIA has been the target of prolonged, sometimes blunderbuss" congressional investigations that uncovered "few illegalities or 'abuses'" but "provided forums for lurid and widely false allegations."[11] Laird added that Congress and the administration overreacted "by subjecting the CIA and FBI to severely restrictive legislation and enfeebling edicts." This enfeeblement was certainly evident in Iran, where our on-the-ground intelligence was far from adequate, and it is doubtless true of other hot spots, including the Soviet Union itself.

Debate Over U.S. Intelligence

During the past decade the domestic debate over foreign intelligence, especially within the media and Congress, has left much to be desired. A principal purpose of this book is to examine that debate, not to determine who was right or wrong but rather to see if the major issues were adequately discussed.

Critics of the CIA have fallen into two broad categories. The hard-core critics saw the CIA as both unprincipled and unchecked—a "rogue elephant," to use the words (later retracted) of Sen. Frank Church (D.-Idaho). Other critics saw the

CIA as an agency with mistakes and blemishes that needed correcting so it could work more effectively.

The hard-core critics tended to divide into two overlapping camps—those who emphasized that the CIA had violated the civil rights of U.S. citizens by subjecting them to "illegal" surveillance and those who charged that CIA covert activity was undertaken to support "reactionary" regimes in the Third World. Frequently the latter group marched under the civil rights banner to appeal to a wider U.S. audience.

In response to this hard-core attack there developed a moderate and low-key defense that acknowledged certain abuses. These defenders, among whom were some present and past intelligence officers and some members of Congress, sought legislation to correct abuses and at the same time to strengthen the effectiveness of the CIA.

The principal participants in the intelligence debate have been members of Congress, the executive branch, various pressure groups, and journalists. The key role of Congress is examined in chapter 2 of this study, and the activities of special lobbies—both the critics and the supporters of foreign intelligence—in chapter 3. The performance of the evening news programs of the three commercial TV networks, ABC, CBS, and NBC, is analyzed in chapter 4.

In a society where the government does not own or control a single newspaper or broadcasting station, the mass media, particularly television, have a powerful influence upon public opinion. The importance of this kind of influence was well understood by Abraham Lincoln, who said: "With public sentiment, nothing can fail; without it nothing can succeed. Consequently, he who molds public sentiment goes deeper than he who enacts statutes or pronounces decisions."[12] Further, the networks under the Fairness Doctrine and their own codes are obligated to give a reasonable opportunity for all views to be heard.

The CIA Charter

The Central Intelligence Agency and the National Security Council were established by the National Security Act of 1947, partly in response to a growing perception of threat from the Soviet Union to U.S. interests in Europe and the Middle East. President Truman and Congress agreed on the need for a peacetime intelligence agency to augment other instruments for safeguarding our security and that of our allies. They also agreed that the CIA should have no domestic police functions. Then and later many thoughtful Americans, including Mr. Truman and Secretary of State Dean Acheson, expressed some concern that the CIA be kept accountable to the President, the Congress, and the American people, recognizing that clandestine overseas activities are often more difficult to monitor and evaluate than those of a more open agency operating on American soil.

The 1947 act specifies that the CIA is to "correlate and evaluate intelligence relating to national security, and provide for the appropriate dissemination of such intelligence within the Government." The CIA should perform such services of "common concern as the National Security Council (NSC) determines can be more efficiently accomplished centrally" and "such other functions and duties related to intelligence affecting the national security" as the NSC "may from time to time direct." The act states that the CIA "shall have no police, subpoena, law enforcement powers or internal security functions." (Excerpts from the National Security Act of 1947 are found in Appendix A.)

According to the act, the "Director of Central Intelligence shall be responsible for protecting intelligence sources and methods from unauthorized disclosure." The CIA act of 1949 further states that the agency is exempted from any "law which requires the publication or disclosure of the organization, functions, names, official titles, salaries, or numbers of personnel employed by the agency."

Operating within this broad yet functionally limited directive, the CIA has three principal tasks, all clearly related to foreign intelligence gathering and operations. In the words of former director William E. Colby, they are:

    1. To produce intelligence judgments, based on information from all sources, for the benefit of policy-makers. The

product is in the form of publications and bulletins on current developments, estimates of future international situations, and in-depth studies on various topics—for example, a study of the origins and growth—over time—of potentially hostile strategic weapons programs.

2. To develop advanced technical equipment to improve the collection and processing of U.S. intelligence.

3. To conduct clandestine operations to collect foreign intelligence, carry out counterintelligence responsibilities abroad, and undertake—when directed—covert foreign political or paramilitary operations.[13]

In its critical review of intelligence since 1975, Congress has directed much of its effort toward rewriting the CIA charter so as to limit the scope of the agency's activities and make it more directly accountable to Congress. It has given almost no attention to the KGB or other hostile intelligence services operating within the United States. Nor has it looked seriously at the need for an effective intelligence establishment or the underlying moral and philosophical aspects of intelligence in a free society.

Toward an Ethic for Responsible Intelligence

Faced with the threats of two expansionist and nuclear-armed Communist powers, the global oil crisis, and many lesser threats around the world, our government would be derelict in its duty to the American people if it did not have the best means available for conducting intelligence, counterintelligence, and covert operations. It would be seriously disadvantaged if it denied itself an instrument available to both its allies and its adversaries. But clandestine intelligence-gathering and covert operations abroad are illegal in the countries where they are carried out. They usually involve an element of deception and are largely hidden from the people whose government conducts them as well as from those of the country where they take place.

Can these operations of the CIA, which serves a democratic government and represents an open society, be morally justified? Can a free society engage in espionage and covert political activities abroad without violating its fundamental values?

The security of the United States and the survival of our free institutions are among our highest values. But there are other values and interests. Ever since America became a world power it has defined its national interests broadly enough to respect—indeed, to include—the rights and legitimate interests of other states. To serve our national interests *and* values, we fought in World War II and thereafter forged a global security system to protect our friends and allies against foreign aggression and subversion. We have supported the genuine self-determination of peoples. We believe our role in World War II was justified both by our objectives and by the actual outcome. Our postwar policies have been equally well intentioned, though some failed to achieve the desired objectives.

Foreign intelligence can be thought of as a form of warfare. Like war, intelligence is an extension of diplomacy. Espionage and covert operations in peacetime, like all foreign policy instruments, are designed to serve basic national interests. Hence all activities of our government in peace or war can and should be judged by the same fundamental political and moral standards.

The doctrine of the "just war" has been an essential part of the Western moral tradition for a thousand years. This doctrine, which defines the proper relation between military force and political responsibility, is deeply rooted in Catholic and Protestant ethics. Although it specifically relates to military conflicts, the just war theory can be applied generally to the problems of "political authority, political community, and political responsibility."[14] In short, this Western view of statecraft has direct relevance to all facets of foreign policy and hence provides a moral yardstick for assessing the justness or rightness of intelligence operations.[15]

The just war theory does not tell us what specific policies a government should undertake. Such decisions must be determined by the nature of the problems faced, the resources available, and other circumstances. But it does advance three standards for determining what is acceptable according to the Western moral tradition: Is the objective of the action just? Are the means employed both just and appropriate? Will the chances for justice be enhanced if the action succeeds?

1. *Is the objective of the action just?* Different actors in the international drama naturally define justice differently, often to suit their own immediate interests. But according to Western norms, embodied in international law and the U.N. Charter, military action taken solely to conquer or subjugate other peoples is illegal and unjust, whether carried out by overt military action or by covert means, while military action designed to defend one's own or an ally's territory against external aggression is justified. Aggressors usually attempt to justify their action by asserting that it was undertaken for self-defense; Hitler so described his attack on Poland in 1939. The situation is often confused and complex, but the distinction between the aggressor and the victim is usually clear, at least to outside observers.

A just war (and, by extension, a just covert operation) may never be undertaken for trivial motives, such as the desire to bolster the ego of a ruling group, or for inappropriate purposes, such as an effort to reform the domestic institutions of other societies.

2. *Are the means employed both just and appropriate?* Just ends can be betrayed by unjust and inappropriate means. The force used must be proportionate to the objective. Excessive force is always wrong, though it is often difficult for a commander to know how much force is required to achieve a specific objective. But in a just cause, such as repelling an invader, the use of too little force is wrong also, because it may prolong the struggle or even enable the aggressor to succeed, thus causing a greater loss of life or a setback for justice and independence, or both.

Certain uses of force are categorically wrong. These include the wanton or purposeless destruction of life or property. Hence the U.S. military code prohibits the deliberate killing of civilians, troops who are surrendering, and prisoners of war and, in fact, requires that these groups be protected and cared for. Because of our principles, the U.S. armed forces in Vietnam went to great lengths, great expense, and substantial risk to spare civilians and help resettle refugees.

For the same reason, the American people were shocked when they heard that U.S. soldiers had killed twenty-two or more unarmed civilians in My Lai in 1968. On the Communist side, in contrast, vengeance or terror killings, such as the cold-blooded murder of at least 2,700 civilians (but perhaps as many as 5,000) in Hue during the 1968 Tet offensive and the shooting at refugee columns in 1975, are rationalized by a peculiar Leninist logic that transforms innocent victims into necessary targets for the success of the "revolution."

Intelligence operations frequently make use of unusual means—such as secrecy, deception, and violence—that are not permissible in normal peacetime pursuits. These extraordinary means present difficult practical and moral problems. In a just war, people are killed, and "peacetime" intelligence is often an extension of warfare, though with far less loss of life.

Specific criticism has been directed against American missionaries and newsmen who have provided information to the CIA. Is there anything intrinsically wrong with this practice if such information helped or was intended to help the more just side to prevail? Journalists and missionaries are also U.S. citizens who have a stake in the survival of freedom. The use of non-CIA employees to provide information should be subjected to the test of just and appropriate means, with the recognition that when given a choice a conscientious policy-maker or citizen should choose the lesser of two evils or the greater of two goods.

3. *Will the chances for justice be enhanced if the action succeeds?* The ultimate practical (and in a real sense moral) test of political behavior is not the ends sought or the means used but the consequences that result directly from the action. (The actor, whether an individual or a government, cannot be held accountable for consequences over which he had no control.) However noble the end and just the means, military or political action is not justified if it has little or no prospect of achieving its objective. Assessing the chances of success or failure is a

moral as well as a practical imperative. A parable of Jesus makes this point: "What king will march to battle against another king, without first sitting down to consider whether with ten thousand men he can face an enemy coming to meet him with twenty thousand? If he cannot, then, long before the enemy approaches, he sends envoys, and asks for terms" (Luke 14:31,32).

The requirement for just consequences can be expressed by this question: If the military action succeeds, will the post-belligerency situation be likely to provide a better chance for peace, security, justice, and freedom than the antecedent situation? Which, for example, would have been the better outcome for World War II, an Allied victory or an Axis victory?

The just war theory is especially pertinent to wartime or other conflict situations in which coercion is an accepted means for one or more parties to pursue its objectives. Since 1945 we have been living in a condition of Cold War in which Moscow, Peking, and their clients employ both peacetime and wartime (i.e., military) means to achieve their expansionist objectives. Confronted by these dangers, the United States, its allies, and other threatened governments are justified in employing unusual and even coercive means, as long as they meet the three "just war" standards. Certainly the past and future activities of the CIA and other U.S. intelligence agencies should be judged by these standards.

Assumptions

It may be useful here to summarize the assumptions, explicit or implicit, in the above analysis:

1. We live in a dangerous world where democratic government, the rule of law, and the survival of freedom are jeopardized by totalitarian states, primarily the Soviet Union and its clients. A score of states in Eastern Europe, East Asia, the Middle East, and Africa have lost their independence as a result of external Communist pressures. The interests of the United States and its allies are also endangered by chaos and conflict in many parts of the Third World.

2. To survive in such a world and to help our allies to survive, the United States needs a vigorous foreign policy, based on strong and ready military power and a wise diplomacy, each supported by an effective U.S. foreign intelligence establishment, including the capability for clandestine collection and covert action.

3. Because the United States is a free and democratic society, our intelligence agencies, like all instruments of government, must be accountable to the President and the Congress, and ultimately to the American people.

4. Any new charter legislation on foreign intelligence agencies should acknowledge the necessity and legitimacy of intelligence. In its oversight function, Congress should seek to keep the agencies responsible but should not impose restrictions that cripple their effectiveness.

5. The debate over intelligence in the past five years has been less than adequate. It has focused on alleged abuses and failures of the CIA and neglected the fundamental question of why and how U.S. foreign intelligence agencies go about their jobs. The press, the Congress, and the executive branch all share responsibility for the unsatisfactory public debate.

6. An effective and responsible foreign intelligence establishment is wholly compatible with the American ethic. It is both politically necessary and morally right to engage in clandestine collection, counterintelligence, and covert political action if these activities meet the standards of the "just war" doctrine—that is, if the ends are just, the means are just and appropriate, and the probable consequences of success would advance the cause of security, justice, and freedom.

This study is limited; it does not attempt to assess the performance of the CIA or any other U.S. intelligence agency. In no sense is it presented as a definitive examination of U.S. foreign intelligence. It is, rather, a study of the *debate* over intelligence in a democratic society. Is this debate grounded in a clear sense of our national purposes and a realistic appreciation of the resources and instruments necessary to fulfill them?

CHAPTER TWO

Congress and Foreign Intelligence

ROY GODSON

FOR THE LAST FIVE YEARS, and to a degree unparalleled since the period immediately after World War II, the U.S. Congress has chosen to involve itself deeply in both the structure and the substance of this country's intelligence services—in what had, up to that time, generally been treated as the "closed world" of foreign intelligence. The very fact of this involvement is unprecedented: it is doubtful that the legislature of any other democratic country, anywhere, or at any time, has ever taken on such a role, or felt the need to do so.

That the Congress has the authority to examine and seek to improve intelligence as it does any other area of American public policy is, of course, beyond question. But one may properly question whether this exercise of authority in the past five years has improved American intelligence and served the national interest. This chapter addresses this question, first by describing the events of the period and then in a preliminary way at least evaluating their impact.

The story begins in earnest in the fall of 1974. Congress was propelled into action by allegations of past and continuing abuses against the civil rights of American citizens by U.S. intelligence agencies. The atmosphere, in large part a carryover from Vietnam and Watergate, was tense and adversary. With the Central Intelligence Agency as the principal target, all the intelligence services were virtually on trial.

Since then, Congress has enacted two significant pieces of legislation affecting U.S. intelligence operations, the clandestine services in particular. A third and even more significant legislative initiative, the so-called Charter, is at this writing still under consideration. Further, Congress has reorganized itself to provide continuing oversight of both the agencies and the processes of U.S. intelligence. Finally, through open hearings, studies, reports—and also occasional leaks—Congress has added to the public record a mass of information about the business of intelligence and its past and present conduct. (It is important to note that this information, while illuminating, is often highly selective: some aspects of intelligence are described in detail, other aspects hardly at all; there is a great deal about intelligence "failures" and next to nothing about "successes"; insofar as foreign intelligence services—the Soviet KGB, for example—abuse the liberties of Americans, this aspect of "foreign" intelligence operations is virtually ignored. And some of the congressional analysis now on the public record may be misleading. More of all this in due course.)

The hostile atmosphere of the mid-1970s has apparently receded, and Congress has become somewhat more supportive of the mission of the intelligence services. Cooperative relationships seem to be developing between the intelligence services and some elements of Congress. Whether this more constructive atmosphere proves to be lasting remains to be seen. Whether it will be conducive to maintaining and even improving this country's intelligence capabilities is also an open question, and certainly the major one.

This chapter is divided into two parts. The first deals with legislation, congressional reorganization and oversight, and congressional efforts to improve the agencies' performance, to reform secrecy and disclosure procedures, and to enhance protection of the civil rights of U.S. citizens. The second part focuses on how Congress through public information and education has affected U.S. foreign intelligence capabilities.

This survey and analysis relies heavily on the hearings records, studies, and reports of the two select investigatory committees—generally referred to by the names of their chairmen as the Church (Frank Church, D-Idaho) Committee in the Senate and the Pike (Otis Pike, D-N.Y.) Committee in the House—and their successors, the two permanent intelligence committees. Other committees in both houses of Congress—Armed Services, Judiciary, and Foreign Relations (in the House, Foreign Affairs, after a brief period as International Relations)—have overlapping jurisdictions in the intelligence area; some of them, and other committees besides, have also had hearings which bore on intelligence. But they have not altered in significant ways the principal actions of the intelligence committees or Congress as a whole.

There will be no attempt to assess systematically the effects of congressional actions on developments abroad. It is virtually impossible for an observer who must necessarily rely on open sources, but some of the relevant data are readily available. In 1975, for example, Congress publicized and then cut off covert U.S. aid to two factions fighting for control of Angola; they subsequently lost to the faction supported by the Soviet Union. The same year, over the strong objections of the CIA, the Pike Committee released information about highly classified clandestine collection methods in use in the Middle East. The committee also appears to have been the source of leaks about covert U.S. relationships with political parties in Italy, the Kurds in Iraq, and King Hussein of Jordan.

The effect of all of this on U.S. credibility with allied intelligence services and potential sources whose confidentiality may no longer be protected is impossible to quantify. At the very least these disclosures and the sensational headlines they provided have not made the task of U.S. intelligence agencies any easier.

The second part of this chapter will be concerned with how Congress has affected this country's intelligence capabilities through public information and education, a role about which the various investigative and permanent committees have been highly vocal. It is a circular affair. By providing the public with information about intelligence, Congress obviously helps to shape public attitudes, which in turn feed back into the policy-making process. If, for example, the public does not understand that counterintelligence is absolutely necessary for the collection of reliable information abroad—as well as for catching spies—the rationale for devoting so much effort to this task will not be understood either. Nor will the public have much sympathy for the use of intrusive techniques of surveillance, particularly as they affect U.S. citizens. Similarly, if the public does not understand that covert action and clandestine collection abroad require elaborate infrastructures which may take years to build, it will not support the continuing investments involved.

Public attitudes also have a direct impact on intelligence capabilities. If the public in this country and abroad comes to believe that covert operations are useless, and that clandestine collection by and from human sources can be replaced by technology, it will be reluctant to assist the agencies when asked to do so. And if the whole business of intelligence is perceived to be immoral as well as useless, it is highly unlikely that talented and dedicated people will take any part in it at all.

Information about our intelligence services reaches the public in two ways which are mutually reinforcing. One is through open congressional hearings, sometimes televised, and the printed reports. Only a few thousand Americans at most pay close attention to these hearings and reports, including journalists, academic specialists, and recognized spokesmen—but they exert influence far beyond their numbers. They appear as expert witnesses before Congress; they teach and produce learned monographs; they counsel with congressional staff, the White House, and the State and Defense departments; and occasionally they lecture at CIA headquarters.

And among their number are those who write most of the major stories about intelligence in the prestige press—which is, of course, the second channel by which information flows from Congress to the majority of the American people. Insofar as the data the press relies on are incomplete or selective or misleading, so too is the coverage—with obvious and significant impact on the reliability of the information which is available to the public. The role of the commercial television networks in this connection is examined in another chapter of this volume.

There is no intention here to assess blame or uncover devious conspiracies. Rather, the point is a simple one. Congress has chosen to make a public issue of the quality and performance of our intelligence services. Congress further claims that it has enabled the American people to "know" a great deal about this complex and rather arcane subject. It is, therefore, both appropriate and necessary to raise some flags about the quality of this information.

PUBLIC POLICY ACTIVITIES

Since 1974, Congress has passed two major pieces of legislation affecting U.S. intelligence activities and has established permanent intelligence committees in the Senate and House to maintain continuing oversight. They are the Hughes-Ryan Amendment (Section 662) to the Foreign Assistance Act of 1974 (PL 93–559) and the Foreign Intelligence Surveillance Act of 1978 (PL 95–511). From 1972 to 1974, Congress considered several other proposals that would have limited or prohibited covert operations by U.S. intelligence agencies, but these were overwhelmingly defeated.

The Hughes-Ryan Amendment

In the aftermath of investigations in 1973 by a Senate Foreign Relations subcommittee on U.S. involvement in Chile, allegations about the CIA's role in Watergate, and the lobbying activities of a number of pressure groups (described in chapter 3), several bills were introduced in the fall of 1974 which would have prohibited covert operations altogether. After these efforts were defeated, Sen. Harold Hughes (D-Iowa) introduced an amendment to the pending Foreign Assistance Act, on October 2, 1974. It provided that no funds under the act could be spent by the CIA for operations not intended solely for the collection of information, unless the President found that each operation was "important" to our national security and so reported in a "timely" fashion to the "appropriate" congressional committees, i.e., Armed Services and Appropriations in both houses. The amendment was considered, altered slightly, and passed the Senate without hearings that same day.

A week later, Rep. Leo Ryan (D-Calif.) of the House Foreign Affairs Committee introduced a similar amendment. The Ryan version added his own committee and Senate Foreign Relations to the four to which the President would be required to report. It also limited its effect to Foreign Assistance Act funds and CIA operations only, not to those of any other intelligence agency. Moreover, it would not apply during a declared war or an exercise of authority under the War Powers Resolution. In their Conference Report of December 17, the Senate receded to the House version, and PL 93-559 as amended was signed into law by the President on December 30, 1974.

Senior CIA officials had tried to get the White House to share their concerns over Hughes-Ryan but without success. Apparently the administration was focusing on other aspects of the Foreign Assistance Act, particularly the compromise on aid to Turkey after the invasion of Cyprus, and did not want to risk upsetting whatever arrangements the State Department had entered into with congressional leaders. Then, too, some members of the White House staff did not regard the new reporting procedures as an especially radical departure: somewhat similar procedures were already in effect for briefing senior members of the House Foreign Affairs Committee about covert operations.[1]

Hughes-Ryan cuts many different ways. For the first time, there is statutory acknowledgment that the CIA might be conducting foreign operations not intended solely for information-gathering. The amendment provides no new or explicit authority; but the CIA has taken the position that it clearly implies that the agency does have the authority to plan and conduct covert operations.[2] The Church Committee, in its Final Report, tends to support this view:

> ... passage [of Hughes-Ryan] did not unambiguously demonstrate a congressional intent to authorize covert action. However, its passage supports the position that Congress has either provided the CIA with implied authority or ratified whatever authority the CIA possessed.[3]

On the other hand, the amendment makes it extremely unlikely that the CIA would attempt to initiate covert action without the clear-cut authorization of the President and the knowledge of Congress. The President has to find that "each such operation is important to national security" and must "describe" its "scope" to Congress in a "timely" manner. Prior to Hughes-Ryan, there were internal executive branch guidelines which restricted CIA activities without prior presidential approval, and almost all of them that have come to public attention appear to have met the guidelines. The new restrictions are much tighter: the President must personally approve each operation and report it to Congress.

By the same token, Hughes-Ryan makes it virtually impossible for the President or Congress to "plausibly deny" any CIA operations which may be uncovered. They are locked in by the new reporting procedures. As a consequence, the President may now be reluctant to authorize activities which could embarrass him later on. At the same time, he can no longer be criticized for not keeping Congress informed.

In any case, Congress now has the opportunity—and even the responsibility which it has consciously assumed—to monitor covert operations closely and systematically. This represents a substantial role reversal. From 1947 until the mid-70s, Congress was apparently satisfied with much less formal procedures. A handful of senior committee chairmen were informed about major operations. Occasionally they requested additional information. Certainly they spent little in the way of staff resources or time on oversight of the intelligence agencies.

When the mood began to shift in the early 1970s, marked in very broad terms by a growing mistrust of the executive, leading members of the House and Senate committees concerned with foreign affairs began to request more and more information about covert operations. The chairmen of the Armed Services and Appropriations committees also recognized that their colleagues wanted to be cut in. One modest response, as noted already, was the institution of briefings—quite limited in scope and detail—for senior members of the House Foreign Affairs Committee.

Hughes-Ryan, by contrast, originally called for six committees to be kept fully informed about presidential findings and CIA operations. The two permanent intelligence committees were later added to the list. These eight committees apparently do not have to be informed before such operations get under way but rather in a "timely" fashion, which has been interpreted to mean near the start or very soon thereafter. They also have to be told the scope and duration of each operation.

It is difficult to tell just how these new arrangements are working. The intelligence committees seem to be satisfied, and so, apparently, is Congress generally. At any rate, there have been no major moves to alter the basic provisions of Hughes-Ryan, and in fact the permanent intelligence committees, through their subcommittees on budget and oversight, exercise even more monitoring of operations than the amendment calls for.

Some journalists who write about covert action do question whether Congress really knows what is going on. They note that Hughes-Ryan does not require the President to report every operation but only those he deems "important." David Wise quotes Sen. Birch Bayh (D-Ind.), chairman of the Senate Intelligence Committee, as saying, "That's the gray area. [CIA director] Turner and I both have other things to do than talk about every little activity or detail." Wise believes that Rep. Les Aspin (D-Wisc.), who heads the House Intelligence Committee's oversight effort, also is worried about what he does not know.[4]

"Presumably among Aspin's concerns," according to Wise, are the generalized "presidential findings" whose existence was disclosed by Seymour Hersh of the *New York Times* on June 1, 1978. He reported that one month after Hughes-Ryan was passed, President Ford issued a series of "worldwide" findings. These declared in advance that all CIA operations dealing with narcotics, terrorism, or counterintelligence were by definition "important" to national security. Hersh also maintained that the Carter administration is using this same "pre-packaged" approach. Wise picks up the thread: "Some members of Congress believe that they use these blanket findings to duck the necessity of reporting on specific operations within those categories." As far as Wise can tell, Aspin does not believe that the CIA is doing this—but he (Aspin) has his "doubts."[5] So far, however, there is no evidence that Congress is not being fully informed.

Indeed, some observers believe that Hughes-Ryan has given Congress *de facto* veto power over covert operations and may have made it impossible for this country to carry out any extensive covert action at all. The critical problem is the dissemination of sensitive information. Under the terms of Hughes-Ryan, in practice some thirty senators and congressmen are in a position to be informed about covert operations. As a practical matter, this means that about twenty-five staff members also share in the information. And, under the rules of the two houses, any individual member who wants to know about such operations may have access to the information as well.

Under these circumstances, almost all former senior CIA officials concerned with clandestine activities maintain covert action has become a thing of the past.[6] There is always the risk of unintentional release of information, which necessarily dooms any covert activity. Then, too, Congress can take direct action and deny funding to a specific operation, as it did in 1975 in Angola. Finally, covert operations can be "vetoed" in effect by a deliberate leak, a device available to any member of Congress.

Perhaps it is too early to assess the full impact of Hughes-Ryan. Experience so far, however, tends to support the view that it has all but ruled out effective covert operations. Most of the major ones which have been brought to the attention of congressional committees pursuant to Hughes-Ryan apparently have become public knowledge.[7]

It can also be argued that the situation is changing. For example, there have been no major unauthorized disclosures about covert operations since the permanent intelligence committees were established. But, as former intelligence officials point out, there has been precious little to leak in the last few years. Ever since Hughes-Ryan was passed, indeed—and for several years before—covert action has been all but defunct.

Foreign Intelligence Surveillance Act (FISA)

Largely as a result of congressional investigations which uncovered what were felt to be abuses in the area of warrantless wiretaps, the Ford and later the Carter administration introduced corrective legislation. In June 1977, the Foreign Intelligence Surveillance Act (S.1566) began a long, arduous course through the legislative process. It was not until the following fall, on October 25, 1978, that the measure was signed into law.

The act is intended to protect the rights of Americans by limiting the use of wiretaps and bugs to cases involving violations of federal law, actual or contemplated, and even then only on a case-by-case finding that the surveillance is legal, i.e., by judicial warrant. To obtain the necessary warrant, newly created Special Judges must be satisfied that the person to be placed under surveillance meets the so-called criminal standard: that is, there must be probable cause to believe that the person is knowingly engaged in clandestine intelligence activities which involve or may involve a violation of the U.S. criminal code; or, that the person commits, prepares to commit, or aids in the preparation of the commission of acts of terrorism or sabotage on behalf of a foreign power. In other words, surveillance is now limited to law enforcement; it cannot legally be used simply to obtain sensitive information. Moreover, in order for a U.S. citizen to be liable to surveillance, that person must not only engage in but must be *aware* of engaging in criminal activity. The act forbids surveillance of those who apparently come innocently into contact with known agents of a foreign power, unless it can be shown that their connection had a direct relation to the illegal intelligence activities of that power.

Furthermore, the act not only leaves it to federal judges to determine whether agents of the United States are adhering to these standards; it also gives them the power to control how the information obtained from a legal surveillance may then be disseminated.

What can we conclude from all this? There is little question but that FISA increases the protection of U.S. citizens—and most foreign visitors and resident aliens as well—from warrantless electronic surveillance, and from the "unnecessary" dissemination of the information so obtained. It also gives U.S. foreign intelligence and counterintelligence officers a firm legal mandate for their operations. It may also represent a genuine attempt—perhaps the first by Congress—to think through and balance the citizen's competing claims to security from foreign powers, their agents, and international terrorists, and to security from electronic surveillance by his own government.

The directors of the CIA, the National Security Agency (NSA), and the State Department's Intelligence Bureau have all stated publicly that the restrictions in the act would not pose unmanageable risks for this country.[8] Former intelligence officers from the Association of Former Intelligence Officers (AFIO), however, have testified that the act would in fact do real damage to U.S. intelligence capabilities.[9] Some members of Congress agreed with this assessment, pointing to several provisions in the act which limit U.S. intelligence without in any way safeguarding the rights of U.S. citizens.

The act, for example, prohibits the surveillance of most foreigners visiting the United States, including high foreign government officials who are not here representing their governments. At any given time hundreds of thousands of foreigners fall into this category. They cannot be put under surveillance to gather what is called "positive intelligence" on foreign developments, or for recruitment purposes—unless, of course, they are about to violate federal law. Nor, under the act, can "members" as contrasted with officials or employees of a "foreign power" be subjected to electronic surveillance in the absence of the "criminal standard." This protects a most interesting group of potential intelligence targets, because a "foreign power" is defined in the act as a political group which is not composed substantially of U.S. citizens—foreign political parties, for example, or trade unions, lobby groups, or student organizations.

Another criticism of the act is that our intelligence agencies are required to destroy at once all electronic intercepts not obviously related to a violation of the law. This confuses intelligence and counterintelligence with law enforcement because apparently innocuous statements exchanged between individuals suspected of engaging in intelligence activities may link up much later with significant intelligence findings. Collecting such a chain of information over time is thus effectively curtailed.

How important are these inhibitions and limitations on our intelligence capabilities? It is hard to say. The Special Court and other features of the act have not yet come into full operation. Most difficult of all is to make the judgment about how much and what kinds of intelligence our agencies might have obtained, had the restrictions not been in force.

It may be even more significant to ask if FISA is a bellwether of what is to come. Some observers believe it is, and that the congruence of forces which produced FISA, ranging from the CIA and the FBI to the American Civil Liberties Union (ACLU) and the Center for National Security Studies (CNSS)—which may have been merely a marriage of convenience, of course, masking deep differences and competing motives among the apparent "allies"—will again become dominant in framing the new Intelligence Charter. Certainly many of the recommendations of the ACLU and CNSS were embodied in the draft which was introduced in the 1978 session of Congress.[10] Others disagree. They believe that the mood in the country is changing and will lead those members of Congress who have always been uncomfortable about the Foreign Intelligence Surveillance Act—along with those who were, as one member put it, "asleep at the wheel"—to go on the offensive against the earlier consensus.

The Intelligence Charter

The draft Charter (S.2525) was introduced in the Senate in February 1978; in March, an identical bill was introduced in the House. They were consciously designed as a "draft" which would be debated and then "modified" for reintroduction in 1979. The 263-page draft—ten times the length of the National

Security Act of 1947 (see Appendix A)—is intended to provide "adequate governance" for our secret intelligence services, beyond the "page or two" presently on the books.

Its Senate authors claim for S.2525 that it provides "both for the finest intelligence system possible and for the protection of the rights of Americans." (All but three members of the Senate Intelligence Committee co-sponsored S.2525—but, again, for mixed motives.) The new Charter, its authors claim, will achieve its goals by establishing "an intelligence structure headed by a Director of National Intelligence; charters for the individual intelligence agencies, setting forth their missions; a requirement that intelligence activities not adversely affect the constitutional rights of Americans; and congressional and other oversight mechanisms to insure the efficient and proper use of the powers granted the intelligence community."[11]

These are the major features of the Charter:

1. The Director of Central Intelligence (DCI), who is presently the nominal head of the entire intelligence community as well as the CIA, would be redesignated as Director of National Intelligence (DNI) with a limit of two six-year terms.

2. The DNI might or might not be the head of the CIA; he would, however, have a strong supervisory role within the intelligence community and become, in effect, the "czar" of all U.S. intelligence.

3. "Special activities" or covert operations would be prescribed as to both initiation and scope, if they might result in mass destruction of food, water, or property, the overthrow of "democratic" governments, or the assassination of foreign leaders. Some of these restrictions could be lifted during a declared war. There would also be stringent requirements for reporting to Congress.

4. Clergy, academics, and journalists could not be used as paid intelligence agents, with some exceptions during a declared war.

5. The foreign intelligence provisions would parallel those of FISA and apply the "criminal standard" to all surveillance of "U.S. persons within the U.S."

6. Specific charters would be adopted for the CIA, FBI, and

NSA. This would be the first statutory base for the NSA, which was established by executive order.

7. Criminal penalties would be established for the unauthorized disclosure of the identities of CIA employees who are lawfully working under cover.

8. In addition to providing specific authorizations and restrictions, sometimes called "legislated standards," S.2525 would greatly strengthen the congressional oversight role. The Attorney General also would have greater responsibility for determining if intelligence activities are legal and taking remedial action if they are not.

Senate hearings on the draft Charter were held in the spring and summer of 1978. Since then the staff of the Intelligence Committee has been engaged in intensive negotiations with all of the interested parties—with the intelligence agencies and the National Security Council, as well as with the pressure groups opposed to major aspects of U.S. intelligence, such as the ACLU and CNSS. Eventually "son of S.2525" is expected to be reintroduced. While it may provide discretionary authority to waive some of the restrictions proposed in the draft under specified circumstances, it will probably retain the thrust of the original bill. The Senate Committee, following the 1978 hearings, said that it still believed in the "basic validity of the bill's approach."

The debate has ranged across a wide spectrum of views. The ACLU, for example, argued that the draft Charter is not restrictive enough to protect the civil rights of Americans. Former intelligence officers claimed, however, that it goes too far—that, even though they accept and indeed welcome the *idea* of a Charter, many of its basic features (and even more specifics) would cripple our foreign intelligence capabilities. Several former CIA directors have agreed with this prognosis. Some former senior officials, those generally who had *not* been involved in the clandestine services, did not.

One of the most systematic critiques of the draft Charter is to be found in the 100-page statement submitted by the Association of Former Intelligence Officers. In its view, the bill is "long on restrictions, short on flexibility to adjust to changing situations and lacking incentives for greater excellence in intelligence." Many of its provisions, the statement went on,

> are ambiguous and would require almost as many lawyers as case officers.... It is out of balance. While designed to empower and guide the entire range of national intelligence activities, it concentrates excessively on a miniscule albeit vital segment of the total effort.

AFIO also argued that S.2525 did not appear to have taken into account "the extant and projected international environment, and the role that intelligence must play in meeting the resultant challenges to the security of the nation."[12]

The debate is doubtless continuing just offstage while everyone concerned awaits the second draft.

Oversight and Reorganization

From 1947 until the mid-70s, Congress by its own choice did not become deeply involved in the intelligence process. Both formally and informally, congressional oversight was applied with a very light hand.[13] What monitoring there was came from two committees in each house. Armed Services and Appropriations served as "watchdogs" over intelligence. These four committees in turn designated a few of their members to do the actual watching.

At their most active, the House "subcommittees" reportedly met with agency officials a half-dozen times a year, spending as much (or as little) as fifteen to twenty hours in oversight. There was little if any record-keeping, formal reporting, or staffing, with the exception of budget review and (later on) Watergate-related matters. The pattern in the Senate was similar. In the 1960s, however, because of overlapping membership, the two "subcommittees" met jointly; during the period when Sen. Richard Russell (D-Ga.) was chairman of both, there was in fact only one. Staff assistance was minimal, and as a general rule there were only two or three meetings a year.

Funds for the CIA were secretly transferred from the appropriations of other agencies. This was managed by the Bureau of the Budget (precursor to the White House Office of

Management and Budget), acting on information provided by the chairmen of the House and Senate Appropriations committees. Amounts and sources of funds were disclosed neither to the full committees nor to Congress as a whole. The informal "subcommittees" did hold closed meetings with intelligence officials to review proposed budgets. Detailed records were made of these proceedings in the House and retained in CIA custody, but apparently no such records were made or retained of comparable Senate proceedings.

From 1947 to 1974, more than 200 bills were introduced which would have increased congressional oversight of the intelligence community, even though little dissatisfaction was expressed openly during those years with the existing arrangements. Some members of the two foreign affairs committees did, however, seek either the creation of a joint oversight committee or an oversight role for themselves. Only two such bills ever reached the floor, and both were defeated. In the late 1960s and early 1970s, provision was made for some members of Congress to sit in on relevant meetings of the Armed Services committees. Then, in 1974, the Hughes-Ryan Amendment, discussed above, was enacted.

In addition to the formal processes, there was considerable informal contact between the intelligence agencies and Congress, and some monitoring of the agencies' activities. The CIA, for example, has asserted that it was in almost daily contact with the chairmen and staff of the four "subcommittees" and, on request, appeared before other committees and briefed individual members. From 1967 to 1972, the CIA says it averaged 23 annual appearances before congressional committees, 80 personal briefings, 1,000 written communications, and 1,450 additional personal contacts with members.

Congress also exercised informal supervision through the confirmation process (of the DCI, for example) and the General Accounting Office. Individual members engaged in other forms of "supervision" as well—as, for example, when Rep. Michael Harrington's (D.-Mass.) letters disclosed the substance of CIA director Colby's secret 1974 testimony on covert action in Chile to "destabilize" the Allende government.

It is difficult, of course, to judge how well Congress was informed—or indeed wanted to be informed—about the activities of the intelligence services during those years. Reportedly Congress did limit some activities, primarily for fiscal reasons, but it never systematically sought a greater oversight role nor did it attempt to make major changes in the structure of U.S. intelligence until the early 1970s. Then the course of affairs changed dramatically.

In the fall of 1974, a subcommittee of Senate Government Operations considered a resolution co-sponsored by Majority Leader Mike Mansfield (D-Mont.) and Sen. Charles Mathias (R-Md.) to establish a select committee to investigate intelligence activities and determine whether congressional oversight needed to be strengthened. In December 1974, Hughes-Ryan was enacted. A few days later, the *New York Times* published articles by Seymour Hersh alleging that the CIA had violated its charter in major ways. Early in 1975, both the House and the Senate did establish select committees to investigate these and similar charges.

The Senate Select Committee to Study Governmental Operations with Respect to Intelligence Activities (the Church Committee) was instructed to consider "the need for improved, strengthened or consolidated oversight of the United States' intelligence activities by the Congress."[14] The ensuing investigation was unique—the first such study of U.S. intelligence and, in all likelihood, the first of any government's intelligence service by its legislature.

It lasted for fifteen months. A staff of 100, including 60 professionals, assisted the 11 committee members in conducting more than 800 interviews and 250 executive hearings and in producing documentation in excess of 110,000 pages.[15] The committee sought the advice of most of the principals who had served in U.S. intelligence since World War II, and outside experts as well. Although it was not permitted to peruse the agencies' files at will, it could and did request a mass of documents; and, as the committee itself reported, there were no "classes of documents which the Committee has not obtained."[16]

The Final Report consisted of six volumes of general findings, including one devoted to "foreign and military intelligence." In addition there were seven volumes of hearings, reports, and studies. These seven volumes included a number of case studies which were "pursued to the best of the Committee's ability and which the Committee believes illuminate the purposes, character and usefulness of the shielded world of intelligence activities."[17]

In the volume on "foreign and military intelligence," the committee concluded that the intelligence services had made "important contributions" to the nation's security and that there is a "continuing need" for all major components of U.S. intelligence, including covert action and counterintelligence. It made the following principal recommendations, most of which, as noted above, were later echoed in the draft Charter:

1. The *National Security Act* should be recast to define the purposes of national intelligence activities, the relationship between Congress and the agencies, the structure, roles, and responsibilities of the intelligence community, and prohibitions and limitations on certain kinds of activities.

2. The *National Security Council* should direct and provide additional policy guidance for intelligence, including collection, counterintelligence, and covert action.

3. The *Director of Central Intelligence,* as principal intelligence adviser to the President, should be divested of direct managerial responsibility for the CIA; instead, he should have increased community-wide authority for coordination of the activities of all of the agencies, including those in the Defense Department.

4. The *Central Intelligence Agency:* to improve quality, national intelligence production should be placed "directly under the DCI" and separated from the clandestine services. Also, the CIA's relations with various kinds of domestic institutions should be strictly limited.

5. *Covert Operations:* only the CIA should be allowed to conduct them, and they should be limited to "extraordinary circumstances when no other means will suffice." Such operations as the subversion of "democratic" governments and as-

sassinations of foreign leaders should be forbidden entirely.

6. *Oversight:* Congress should authorize the national intelligence budget annually and, in addition to being informed about them, should approve all covert operations. The roles of the U.S. Attorney General and CIA's General Counsel and Inspector General also should be broadened to prevent abuses and illegal activities.

In the second volume of its Final Report, "The Rights of Americans," the Church Committee confirmed to its satisfaction that there had been wiretapping, surveillance, and mail openings within the United States against U.S. citizens; that the intelligence agencies had engaged in disruptive acts against domestic political dissidents; and that the United States had intervened or attempted to intervene in the political processes of other countries to an extent apparently unknown to the congressional oversight committees.

Even before the Final Report had been prepared, the Senate Government Operations Committee held hearings and, in February 1976, unanimously reported out S.Res. 400 to establish a standing committee with authorization and oversight jurisdiction over intelligence. In April, the Church Committee supported this proposal.[18] After additional hearings and considerable legislative jockeying, an amended version of S.Res. 400 (the so-called Cannon Compromise) passed the Senate on May 19, 1976, by a vote of 77 to 22.

Under the terms of the resolution, a new standing Committee on Intelligence was given *exclusive* jurisdiction over the CIA and the DCI (except for the broader reporting procedures under Hughes-Ryan) and *shared* jurisdiction over the Defense Intelligence Agency, the State Department's Intelligence and Research Bureau, and the FBI, with the Armed Services, Foreign Relations, and Judiciary committees. It also required annual authorizations for the principal components of the intelligence community.

The new Senate Intelligence Committee was given the following charge: (1) to oversee and make continuing studies of U.S. intelligence and submit to the Senate appropriate reports and legislative recommendations; (2) to ensure that the agencies provide the executive and legislature with the informed and timely intelligence needed to make sound decisions affecting the nation's security; (3) to provide "vigilant" oversight to ensure that all intelligence activities conform to the constitution and laws of the United States; and (4) to study the intelligence process in all of its aspects, including planning, gathering, use, security, and dissemination.

The committee was set up from the start as a bipartisan body with fifteen members, eight Democrats and seven Republicans, with the Senate Majority and Minority Leaders *ex officio*. There are six subcommittees (Intelligence and the Rights of Americans; Budget and Authorization; Collection, Production and Quality; Charters and Guidelines; Secrecy and Disclosure; and Special Investigations) with a staff of about forty-five, twenty-three of whom are professionals trained in various social science and other disciplines, including that of intelligence. Each member nominates one professional, subject to approval by a majority of the committee, who then works for the entire committee under Staff Director William G. Miller, an alumnus of the Church Committee senior staff. With the approval of the chairman and a committee majority, Miller also has hired several additional staff professionals. No senator may serve on the committee for more than eight consecutive years, and no staff member for more than six.

The committee's own security rules are tight. Staff members sign secrecy agreements and receive FBI clearances. Classified documents are given special care and handling, and access is controlled by a specific "need to know." The rules of the Senate provide, however, that the committee may make classified material in its possession available on request to any senator of any committee. This means that material prepared and classified with the intent that access be limited to a small number of trained and cleared intelligence professionals is now available to committee members and, potentially, to an even larger number of senators who have undergone none of the intensive scrutiny normally required for a security clearance. Election and a self-defined "need to know" are accepted as equivalents of formal clearance.

Moreover, cleared staff members not only have a mandate to peruse documents at the committee's office, but also they are free to make formal visits to the CIA and other agencies. While there are some places that are off limits without special clearances, the very breadth of the committee's charge makes a significant range of classified information available to the staff on request. There are no inherent limits on congressional access, only those which are imposed by intelligence officials. Indeed, it is fair to say that some staff members have fuller access to sensitive information than do most intelligence officers. The latter operate generally in a highly compartmentalized context and on the basis of quite restrictive "need to know" criteria; some of the congressional staff, in contrast, can range widely across the entire intelligence horizon. Further, the committee, with the approval of the Senate, is free to publish any information in its possession—including classified material—over the objections of the executive.

Following the lead of the Senate, the House undertook a broad investigation of intelligence and in February 1975 established its Select Committee to investigate legislative and executive oversight of foreign intelligence; overt and covert activities; the "collection, analysis, use and cost of the intelligence components of the U.S. government"; and "allegations of improper activities."[19]

But the House Committee ran into heavy seas. Dissension among the Democratic members became public knowledge, and on June 12, 1975, Chairman Lucien Nedzi (D-Mich.) resigned. In July, the committee was reconstituted with Rep. Otis Pike (D-N.Y.) as chairman. The Pike Committee, with about half as many staff members as its Senate counterpart, held extensive public hearings which again aroused controversy. The executive branch was disturbed by congressional access to information and witnesses, and by the committee's deliberate publication of classified material.

The controversy became so intense that on January 29, 1976, the full House voted 246 to 124 to block the release of the Pike Committee's Report unless the President was willing to certify that its release would not adversely affect U.S. foreign intelligence. (A draft of the report was subsequently leaked. With CBS news correspondent Daniel Schorr acting as midwife, it was published in the *Village Voice*.) The committee did, however, present its recommendations to the House early in February. It proposed the creation of a standing committee on intelligence with "exclusive jurisdiction for budget authorization for all intelligence activities and . . . all covert action operations." Two committee members presented minority views, recommending instead the creation of a Joint House-Senate Intelligence Committee.

It was not until July 1976—and only after the personal intercession of House Speaker Tip O'Neill and President Carter—that the House Rules Committee reported favorably on H.Res. 658, patterned largely on S.Res. 400. Under its terms, a Permanent Committee on Intelligence would be established, with essentially the same jurisdictions and procedures as the Senate Committee. After a stormy floor debate, the committee was established by a vote of 227 to 171.

The House Committee's mandate is similar to that of the Senate's, and it has created similar subcommittees: Program and Budget; Legislation; Oversight; and Evaluation and Performance. The committee has a professional staff of fourteen, selected in the same manner as the Senate staff, and a support staff of thirteen.

The rules of the House, as in the Senate, permit any member to peruse the reports and documents of any committee. (This rule enabled Rep. Michael Harrington [D.-Mass.] to secure access to DCI Colby's closed-hearing testimony on covert operations in Chile and later to disseminate information drawn from that testimony.)

The Permanent Intelligence Committees

The two permanent committees by early 1979 have issued one report each. The Senate Committee's first report was published in May 1977, and, according to press spokesman Spencer Davis, the second was supposed to appear the spring of 1979.[20] In its first brief report, the committee concluded that the intelligence agencies were basically under control by the President and DCI, and fully accountable to Congress. With the oversight procedures in effect, and the enactment of necessary legislation, it was the committee's judgment that widespread abuses of power were a thing of the past.[21] In its view, the agencies had been forthcoming, the committee had been informed of every covert operation requiring a presidential finding prior to implementation, and it had voted formally on all covert operations in the authorizations for general intelligence activities.

The House Committee issued its first report in October 1978. This even briefer document came to much the same conclusion: for "the first time . . . a continuous monitoring of the intelligence operations had been performed by a full Committee of the House. . . ."[22]

After five years of contention, Congress appears to be satisfied that it is performing a proper and effective oversight role. The formal mechanisms have been systematized and strengthened. Congress is now informed about every major aspect of the intelligence process and, through its authorizations, passes on them all.

Informal procedures continue to invest a few congressional leaders with preponderant influence, particularly the committee and subcommittee chairmen and key staff members. At their option, these individuals probably can veto many of the intelligence activities of which they have knowledge. There is nothing unusual about this kind of influence. In all areas of public policy, the perception of what "Congress wants" on a day-to-day basis is generally a reflection of the views of committee chairmen and key staff. The agencies can object but can hardly demand formal committee votes. Or they can work behind the scenes and, by prevailing on a few influential committee members, attempt to have an uncooperative chairman overruled. But this is unwieldy and full of risks. Thus the new arrangements permit Congress to influence U.S. foreign intelligence activities as it never has before.

Whether this influence will persist in the long term is by no means clear. Studies of congressional oversight in general suggest that when other pressing issues arise, and there is little political mileage to be gained from constant and relatively anonymous diversion of time and energy, most members of Congress do not perform as conscientious overseers—nor do they remain so deeply involved in initiating reforms.[23] Nevertheless, the recent reorganization of the intelligence oversight process, the sizable staff involved, and the inherent "sex appeal" of the issues themselves will combine to guarantee a measure of continuing scrutiny. But once the Charter is enacted—if it is, and whatever degree of restrictions it imposes—and once the political limelight shifts, the future behavior of Congress is problematic.

Also uncertain is how much Congress will do to improve rather than merely monitor U.S. intelligence. A great deal will depend on the prevailing political climate, both at home and abroad, and on the intensity of congressional involvement in national security policy generally. Intelligence is no easy discipline to master. Thus, although it has created the opportunity for itself, Congress may find it very difficult to devise ways of improving collection, analysis, counterintelligence, and covert action capabilities.

Evaluation, Quality, and Performance

Both intelligence committees have subcommittees dealing with the quality of U.S. intelligence, but there have been few reports and no hearings on this vital issue—at least not in public view. Moreover, interviews with members and staff indicate that almost all major actions have been reported in published documents.

Using the Church Committee's case-study approach, the Senate Committee has explored three problems relating to intelligence analysis: there have also been some staff interviews on other comparable problems. It is of some interest that all of these cases were studied only *after* they had become the subjects of press reports and public controversy. The committee has never examined counterintelligence or covert action in any systematic way.

The three cases are: "U.S. Intelligence Analysis and the

Oil Issues, 1973–1974," "The National Intelligence Estimate—A-B Team Episode Concerning Soviet Strategic Capability and Objectives," and "The Soviet Oil Situation: An Evaluation of CIA Analysis of Soviet Oil Production." The published reports present pertinent critiques and find some positive aspects in the CIA's analyses, but unfortunately the committee did not propose general or specific measures to improve performance.

The House Committee has taken a somewhat different approach—and may have accomplished more.[24] It has focused in the main on issues of organization and management as they affect the value of intelligence to its users. The committee also has examined National Intelligence Estimates and reports from specific trouble spots. While it found the reporting generally responsive to user requirements, it concluded that "there may be considerable room for improvement—especially in such areas as estimating, forecasting, and trend analysis reporting."

Furthermore, the committee criticized the agencies for various faults and studied several topics in depth. On the basis of one such study, on "Warning," the committee found that analysis could be improved and better integrated with policy formulation. "By sharing the findings of the subcommittee with the Executive Branch, and entering into a dialogue on these issues," its report went on, "a positive step" was taken to correct a weakness in our warning systems. That step, apparently, was the creation of a National Intelligence Officer for Warning, designated "largely in response to criticisms by the Committee." While the creation of one position fell short of the full range of the committee's concerns, "the newly instituted procedures hold promise for improving analysis."

The House Committee also issued a brief report on one "intelligence failure"—an eight-page study, "Iran: Evaluation of U.S. Intelligence Performance Prior to November 1978." The report is a single case study about a subject that had already received extensive publicity. The committee attributed the failure of American policy to both the intelligence community and the users of intelligence. It concluded with several suggestions for changes in analytical procedures and the structure of the

DCI's office. The committee also held five days of closed hearings on terrorism and the U.S. capacity to deal with it.

Both committees have expressed concern about the possible weakening of U.S. counterintelligence and counterterrorism programs as a result of the McGovern Amendment to the Foreign Relations Authorization Act of 1978. This amendment enables certain aliens, hitherto barred from the United States, to enter the country even when the FBI advises against it on the ground that they might well be involved in espionage or terrorist activities.

Program and Budget

The resolutions creating the permanent intelligence committees gave them the authority to review, evaluate, and set limits on the annual budgets of the intelligence agencies and to monitor their expenditures. The two committees' powers differ somewhat, but each shares its power with the Armed Services Committee in its chamber. For the first time in U.S. history, in 1978 Congress specifically authorized appropriations for all aspects of intelligence, including a project review of covert action.

The classified nature of intelligence activities, the committees have asserted, prevents them from releasing the details of their budgetary analyses and reports. But they seem to have worked hard on programs and budgets. For fiscal year 1979, the House subcommittee heard fifty-five hours of testimony from no fewer than twenty witnesses. It also held two days of hearings on whether to make public the overall figure for the intelligence budget. The Senate Committee held similar hearings and examined some 2,000 pages of budget justifications and a number of special studies.

The committees' reviews, according to their annual reports, covered the full range of intelligence activities and their management by the agencies. Each agency's budget was examined, and duplications were searched out. The committees also considered proposals for high-technology collection systems which require long lead times for development. They concluded that, on the whole, intelligence is well managed, there is room for improvement, and duplication could be avoided, particularly between the CIA and the Defense Department. The totals authorized were close to those requested by the President—with some cuts and some additions.

Then came the question of whether to go public with the total appropriation. The House Committee was firmly against disclosure, but the Senate Committee voted 9 to 8 for public release. Chairman Birch Bayh (D-Ind.) and the Senate leadership apparently decided either that the Senate would reverse the committee's judgment or, if not, that the Senate would be exposed to needless criticism in the early days of its new oversight role. In any event, the figures were not released.

The issue is likely to surface again. Certainly the Senate Committee chairman and many members of his committee want to publish the figures. The House Committee also concluded that it "had to determine whether a reassessment of its position is required."[25]

Secrecy, Disclosure, and Classification

In 1977, the Senate Committee established a subcommittee to review the complex matters of secrecy, disclosure, and classification. This was the first such systematic effort by Congress since 1917. The relevant statutes had been enacted in the highly charged atmosphere of World War I and then supplemented by executive orders and regulations in the post-World War II period. The House followed the Senate's lead in 1978.

The committees said they wanted to determine whether the existing laws were adequate to maintain legitimate secrecy, whether they were so ambiguous that they could be used to stifle freedom of expression, and whether the classification rules permitted excessive secrecy and created incentives to violate the law.

Senate hearings were held early in 1978 on the impact of the secrecy laws on the administration of justice in national security cases—i.e., where investigations and prosecutions had been frustrated by claims of national security. In its findings, the committee concluded (1) that there had been a major failure on the government's part to take action in cases of unauthorized disclosure because of fears of further damage to national security, and (2) that several immediate steps could be taken by the executive to enhance the administration of the existing statutes, as Congress determined the need for major revisions. The House began similar hearings and the consideration of a bill early in 1979.

But neither house has acted with a sense of urgency on these matters. The Ford administration's proposed revisions of the secrecy laws died in committee in 1976. The Senate Committee has been studying the subject for two years and has not yet produced comprehensive legislation—beyond those aspects of the problem which are dealt with in the draft Charter.

Oversight and the Rights of Americans

Oversight and the civil rights of U.S. citizens remain a principal concern of the two intelligence committees. They now seem to believe they are in a position to monitor the intelligence agencies—and to prevent such abuses of the rights of Americans as may have occurred in the past. The committee chairmen maintain that there is now adequate oversight, although they sometimes point out that the process is still in evolution.[26] Two important targets have been the abuse of the rights of Americans by "friendly" foreign intelligence services and the CIA's use of the media.

In June 1978, the Senate Committee issued a report on the activities of one friendly service, the South Korean CIA. The report concluded that our government should, in addition to its counterintelligence efforts aimed at hostile intelligence services, step up its monitoring of friendly services; should be aware of the aspirations, agents, and targets of these services; and should prevent "improper activities" by them in this country.

The report's introduction noted that Soviet and other hostile services "pose a more direct threat" to U.S. security and the infringement of civil rights "than do a few random, albeit intensive operations of friendly countries."²⁷ Apart from this fleeting reference, however, the committee has paid no attention to such threats—and this in spite of the fact that one of its members, Daniel P. Moynihan (D-N.Y.), has repeatedly cited massive violations of American civil rights by Soviet electronic interceptions. Other observers have pointed to Soviet, Cuban, and East European operations which affect everyday life in the United States. No hearings have been scheduled on this vital problem. No reports have been prepared. No legislation is being considered.

The House Committee also has taken a rather narrow view of the matter. It has produced a classified report on U.S. covert operations and has begun to study the relationships between the CIA and various private institutions—so far, only the media. Six days of hearings were held to determine what *is* the proper relationship, if any, and while the hearings may have illuminated an obscure subject, they have produced no tangible results.

Moreover, the hearings were limited to *our* government's relations with the American media. They did not cover other governments' secret relations with the American media in the United States or such activities abroad as are targeted to or feed back into this country. At the request of Rep. John Ashbrook (R-Ohio), however, the CIA did prepare an analysis of how the Soviet Union manipulates the foreign media and other non-governmental institutions abroad. How U.S. citizens might be affected by comparable activities in this country apparently has not been of sufficient interest to engage the committee's attention.

Indeed, as the headlines fade and other issues come to the fore, it is an open question whether Congress will maintain even its present interest in these matters. Rep. Les Aspin (D-Wisc.), who heads the oversight subcommittee in the House, seems also to wonder:

> A lot of what we do is secret. Because of it, there is very little political mileage for a Congressman to expend a lot of time in this area. It's a thankless task. . . . You're caught between the right and left. You're not getting any brownie points from

your constituents. They want to know what you're doing. For all these reasons, oversight is a real sonofabitch.[28]

Educating the Public

Congressional Hearings and Reports

If one of the responsibilities of Congress is to provide a fair and balanced picture of the public issues it addresses, the American people have not been particularly well served by the congressional debate on foreign intelligence since 1974. Scholars, journalists, and the public generally can learn a great deal from the protracted hearings and voluminous reports, but the considerable information they contain was made less useful by serious omissions as well as inconsistencies.

There were several reasons for this. One was the need for secrecy, which resulted in deletions of information passed on to the public by the Congress. But some distortions stemmed from inadvertent or intentional committee decisions to focus on certain aspects of the intelligence question and *not* to focus on others. Whether through design or accident, the result was an incomplete picture of the issues at stake.

Clearly, there is a point at which public education comes into conflict with the requirements of secrecy, and locating that point is itself an issue of controversy. (This consideration bears, to be sure, on the wisdom of the entire course of congressional action over the last five years, and not just on the contents of the public record.) Nevertheless, Congress could have gone much further to educate the public about important aspects of intelligence which received only cursory treatment.

This conclusion emerges from a detailed qualitative analysis of the hearings and reports of the four major congressional committees—the Church and Pike committees and their permanent successors. It is clear, for that matter, even from a quite broad-brush quantitative analysis—merely from counting the pages in the hearings and reports which are devoted to particular subjects.

Although it was not always possible to distinguish clearly

CONGRESS AND FOREIGN INTELLIGENCE 49

which material fell into which category, six categories were established for examination. Four were defined by the major components of foreign intelligence: analysis of intelligence data, clandestine collection, covert action, and counterintelligence. A fifth category dealt with the rights of Americans, congressional oversight, and budgetary matters. The sixth was general, including DCI nominations, the committees' annual reports, and some items that did not fit elsewhere.

TABLE 1

DISTRIBUTION OF INTELLIGENCE ISSUES: 1975–1979

From January 1975 to March 1979, the four major congressional committees dealing with foreign intelligence—the Church and Pike committees and their permanent successors—produced 7,093 pages of hearings and reports for the public record.* The distribution of issues addressed is given by committee and by pages.

ISSUE	CHURCH COMM.	PIKE COMM.	SENATE COMM.	HOUSE COMM.	TOTALS No.	%
1. Analysis and collection	67	240	35	8	350	4.9
2. Clandestine collection	12	....	....	....	12	.2
3. Covert action	791	....	....	....	791	11.1
4. Counterintelligence	20	....	....	....	20	.3
5. Rights of Americans	1,523	667	1,514	1,288	4,992	70.4
6. Other	563	....	293	72	928	13.1
TOTAL	2,976	907	1,842	1,368	7,093	100.0

*The permanent Senate Intelligence Committee also produced another hearing of 1,101 pages on the draft Charter S.2525. Although the hearing in major part concerned the rights of Americans, it also was concerned with the other issues categorized above and could probably be divided almost equally through the six categories. To simplify the chart, and because it in no way alters the major conclusion, the hearing has not been included in the table above.

As table 1 shows, the sharpest distinction is between category five, on the one hand, and categories two, three, and four, on the other hand. The public can learn relatively little from this record about clandestine collection, covert action, or counterintelligence, and only slightly more about some of the problems relating to analysis. But in sheer volume at least, it can learn a great deal about category five—how the rights of Americans were allegedly, or in fact, abused by their own government, and about congressional oversight and budgetary matters.

Both investigatory committees began with ambitious goals, and the Church Committee in particular claims largely to have fulfilled them:

> The information which is presented in this report is a *reasonably complete picture* of the intelligence activities undertaken by the United States, and the problems that such activities pose for constitutional government.[29]

The Pike Committee in the House had similar goals.[30] In the end, of course, the House declined to publish the committee's final report, but as noted above, most of the draft report appeared in the *Village Voice*. The entire draft text was later reprinted by a radical British publishing house.[31]

The Church Committee report focused primarily on bureaucratic and organizational issues—only rarely on the need for sound intelligence or the difficulty of obtaining it. Over 80 per cent of the U.S. intelligence budget is spent by the Defense Department; yet only 45 pages of a 500-page report are devoted to defense intelligence. The CIA receives about 200 pages, and the State Department's Intelligence and Research Bureau gets only 15.

The unauthorized version of the Pike Committee report describes the committee's oversight experience (70 pages) and its investigative record (151 pages) and devotes most of the balance of its 284 pages to recommendations for the future. The section on the quality of intelligence is possibly the most interesting: it describes nine "representative" intelligence failures; there is no mention of successes. The section on political risks is also highly selective. It includes brief reports on political influence being exerted on the agencies—in connection with the SALT negotiations, for example—and on clandestine collection and domestic intelligence-gathering. The only real attempt at detailed analysis is a study of the top-level executive branch approval process for covert operations from 1965 to 1975 and three relevant case histories.

Neither report devotes much systematic attention to the agencies' analytical capabilities or what might be done to improve them. The Church report spends 20 pages out of 500 on finished intelligence, which it says it considers to be the "main purpose of the intelligence system."[32] But most of these 20 pages are taken up with explanations of the functions of various parts of the bureaucracy. In a comparable section of the Pike report, six more "failures" are analyzed—e.g., the Yom Kippur War of 1973 and the Tet Offensive of 1968—drawn largely from the CIA's own post-mortems. While these cases are inherently interesting, the committee never makes clear what criteria were used for their selection or what it might have been seeking to achieve with its analysis. Nor does it place these case studies in the context of U.S. intelligence efforts overall. Do they represent one in ten, or one in a hundred, or one in a thousand, per day or month or year?

The reports devote even less attention to the problems and requirements of clandestine collection. In the Church report collection is discussed in passing in a chapter on the history of the CIA. The Pike report also touches on the subject in both the performance and risks sections. Possibly because of the CIA's request not to publish a chapter on espionage, which the Church Committee honored, it was decided not to publish information on this subject elsewhere in the report. Neither committee draws major conclusions about clandestine collection. One interesting generalization, however, emerges from the Pike Committee's six "failure" case studies—greater reliance on technical collection alone will not improve collection or analysis. But the need for a proper mix of technical and human source collection, using both overt and clandestine methods, is nowhere discussed.

The Church report expressed a fleeting concern that some clandestine activities in the past may have violated international law or the laws of other countries. By definition, espionage and many other aspects of intelligence are indeed unlawful by both standards. Whatever international norms there may be governing espionage and covert operations have been violated so often by just about every civilized government, and some not so civilized, that their viability and even their existence can be questioned. Despite its misgivings, the Church Committee calls unabashedly for the continuation of counterintelligence, which is often as unlawful as espionage. But the committee did not examine either espionage or counterintelligence in the larger context of the other components of an effective intelligence service with a view to how the intelligence community as a whole could better serve the nation's security.

To the sins of omission over analysis and clandestine collection must be added sins of commission. The Church Committee apparently concluded that the CIA has tended to be dominated by the clandestine services—by the Directorate for Plans (DDP), which in 1973 was renamed the Directorate for Operations (DDO). Moreover, within the clandestine services, the covert action specialists rather than the clandestine collectors seem generally to have been in the driver's seat—or so the report suggests. By implication, the analytical branches in the Directorate for Intelligence (DDI), and even the clandestine collectors, have not received adequate emphasis and support. The report seems to base these conclusions on several factors, among them: (1) the espionage and counterintelligence arms failed to provide the DDI with sufficient quality information; and (2) budget figures, manpower strength, the background of the DCIs, and allegations about how they spent their time all tend to point toward these conclusions.

The contention that the DDP failed to supply enough information can be substantiated only if it is assumed that the DDI was supposed to, or expected to, receive a major part of its raw material from this source. But such has never been the case. The product of clandestine collection may sometimes provide a crucial link in the analytical chain; but it was never meant to be quantitatively large or the major source for information which might also be obtained from more open sources. Clandestine collection was meant to serve as a supplement—providing at most some 5–10 per cent of the data from the more open areas of the world, and 10–20 per cent from the less accessible areas. To construe the role of the DDP as mainly that of the DDI's information collector, simply because they are complementary parts of the same umbrella organization, is a fundamental misreading of how the U.S. intelligence system was organized.

Role of Covert Action

The second conclusion—that covert action tended to dominate collection, counterintelligence, and analysis—also is not adequately substantiated. Budget figures do tend to point in this direction. But they are misleading: covert action is expensive; *of necessity* it costs more than espionage or counterintelligence. Operations like Radio Free Europe and Radio Liberty, paramilitary activities, and support for political parties and the media all involve large expenditures.

Another misleading argument in the report moves from the fact that DDP manpower strength increased by 2,000 from 1953 to 1961, to a total of 8,200—or 9,200 including administrative support. (All these figures are drawn from the report itself.) But the report draws no conclusion from its own citation of DDP manpower of 5,800 in 1970—which would mean a ten-year decrease of 2,400, or about 30 per cent. If the DDP was so dominant throughout the 1960s, why was it declining in strength? And why was it declining even in the face of the manpower demands of the Vietnam War?

A third argument which purports to demonstrate the dominance of the DDP is that the DCIs were DDP-oriented or had risen to the top through DDP ranks. Of the eight DCIs who served from 1947 to 1975, only two in fact—Richard Helms and William Colby—were even CIA careerists. Both of them, it is true, did come up through the DDP; and Allen Dulles, the longest serving of all DCIs, was reputed to have a particular interest in the work of the DDP. But it is also true that none of the DCIs who presided over the DDP's growth had any background there. Indeed, it was precisely the DDP careerists, Helms and Colby, who were serving as DCI while the DDP was falling off in strength.

Nor is much evidence presented to substantiate the contention that DCIs were generally preoccupied with the clandestine services. The evidence that *is* presented seems very thin. For example, DCI John McCone, according to an unnamed former staff assistant, allegedly spent 90 per cent of his time on DDP matters. Yet, elsewhere in the report, McCone is credited with improving the CIA's intelligence product; developing new technical collection systems in overhead reconnaissance and coordinating procedures with the Air Force; establishing the office of National Intelligence Programs Evaluation, the first major effort by a DCI in the area of intelligence community coordination; creating the new Directorate for Science and Technology; and reorganizing the Office of the Director—truly a herculean effort if accomplished in only 10 per cent of his time! This line of argument is, in any event, somewhat simplistic. How an effective executive allocates time is usually a function of which aspects of the total organization demand close attention—in the case of a DCI, which aspects (involving as they do grave risks to personnel and the nation's very existence) demand tight personal control. In view of the general thrust of its investigations, one might have expected the Church Committee to *insist* that DCIs concentrate on DDP matters, and not to be critical of such concentration.

Compared to the treatment of clandestine collection and counterintelligence, the information the Church Committee provides on covert action is voluminous. Its report represents one of the most thorough discussions of the subject ever to be made public. When it is combined with Volume VII of the hearings and the report on "Covert Action in Chile," the result is a virtual handbook or primer on methods of covert political action, encompassing electoral support, propaganda, and media influence. There is nothing quite comparable on paramilitary activities, although the committee's description of Operation MONGOOSE against Castro (in the report on "Alleged Assassination Plots Involving Foreign Leaders") may contain the basic outlines of one such operation.

Nevertheless, the coverage of covert activities is flawed and uneven. Both reports concentrate on failures. There is barely a hint that covert action was ever used successfully. The sequence of operations which was so instrumental in preventing

Soviet-controlled Communist parties from dominating Western Europe in the post-World War II period, for example, is hardly mentioned. Yet this was probably the most extensive and the most successful covert action which the U.S. government has ever mounted—and this and other such examples are essential to a genuine public understanding of the risks and costs, *and the benefits,* of this major instrument of national security policy. It would also seem essential to the public's understanding to describe the massive covert operations of the Soviet Union (its manipulation of Communist parties in the West, for example) against which U.S. actions were so often targeted.

Furthermore, both reports tend to leave the impression that covert operations were undertaken in a policy vacuum, uncoordinated with other elements of the CIA or of the U.S. government generally. Except for one brief comment by Henry Kissinger, there is almost no discussion of covert action—in its typical mode—as a supplement and an adjunct to diplomatic action, as one element within a larger scheme. The impression is left that the CIA and the executive believed that covert action would be a panacea for complex foreign policy problems, or that wild-eyed adventurers led this country into international crises largely of their own making.

The Church report also claims that, prior to the 1970s, there were no internal CIA guidelines for submitting covert action proposals to top executive branch levels for approval. Such guidelines certainly existed at least as early as the late 1950s, and were in effect at least through the 1960s. During the 1960s all covert operations costing $25,000 or more had to have Special Group (i.e., National Security Council) approval.[33]

It appears that the Church Committee is opposed to maintaining a covert action infrastructure in foreign countries for fear that it might get out of control—that it might take on a life of its own and invent projects simply to keep busy. Possibly this is a danger. But the obverse, nowhere discussed in the report, is that some actions might have failed, or never have been initiated, because of insufficient leadtime to acquire the necessary covert assets. The attentive public is virtually driven to conclude that an infrastructure is both dangerous and unnecessary. Yet the committee concedes that covert action may be necessary in extreme circumstances.

Finally, the Church report clearly is concerned more with abuses, or potential abuses, than with building and maintaining a first-rate covert action capability. The report has little or no discussion of improving our future capability. It only recommends that various restrictions be imposed—by Congress, by the executive, and by the CIA itself.

Counterintelligence is given quite short shrift in the Church report and no specific, pinpointed attention at all in the Pike report. In all, there is a fifteen-page chapter on counterintelligence, a six-page appendix on Soviet intelligence (both in the Church report), and fleeting references to counterintelligence in other sections of both reports. They provide very limited information about an absolutely vital aspect of intelligence, perhaps the most secret and sensitive there is, and one that it is particularly difficult for laymen to comprehend. Because of the need for extreme secrecy, most of what the Church Committee said about counterintelligence is classified.

Indeed, it is difficult to quantify the subject by numbers of personnel and cases and the funds involved. Espionage cases which are taken to court in this country, foreign officials declared *non grata* and expelled from the United States, and similar data from abroad, particularly in friendly countries, represent only the tip of a massive iceberg.

And even though it is possible to estimate the number of fulltime personnel in the CIA's counterintelligence or CI staff (based on the size of the DDO overall) and the FBI's CI staff, this still would not give a complete picture of CI activity and its importance. Other sections also perform counterintelligence functions, although we have no man-year figures for their time. In operations, research, internal review, training, and liaison with foreign counterintelligence services, the CI staffs and other components of the intelligence services play different but related roles.

With so little knowledge of this most secret of secret activities, it is difficult to assess its quality and significance. Nevertheless, it is quite obvious that if the United States is deceived or penetrated to any substantial extent, U.S. interests are significantly and dangerously jeopardized. If the U.S. intelligence services can successfully deceive and penetrate hostile states, U.S. interests are enhanced. It is unfortunate that, at the very least, broad generalizations of this sort were not included in the reports. It is also unfortunate that the public was not informed about some of the anticipated requirements for the future.

The publications of the two intelligence committees which succeeded the Church and Pike committees have not added a great deal of new public information. So far, these studies have focused on problems of analysis. They consist for the most part of unclassified summaries of four episodes. They make major recommendations but with almost none of the supporting data which would make it possible to evaluate their conclusions.

The first Senate report, in 1977, assessed U.S. intelligence analysis of the oil crisis of 1973–74. It concluded that specialized public sources may have equaled or even exceeded the performance of the intelligence community; that there was a wealth of raw data providing strong indications of shifts in Saudi policy; that analysts underutilized the available field data; that quantity rather than quality of analysis was stressed; and that the analysts did not adequately integrate political and economic factors.

The report notes that the analysts in the DDI (now the National Foreign Assessment Center or NFAC) preferred short summary field reports rather than more detailed but fragmentary reports. It is somewhat surprising that the Intelligence Committee did not recommend, as the Church Committee had, that the DDO collectors be more responsive to the analysts. Neither committee, however, called attention to the fact that the CIA's DDO is a collection service for *all* customers and analysts throughout the intelligence community, and not just for the CIA. The DDO and NFAC happen to be under the same organizational umbrella. But any change in the relationship between DDO collectors and NFAC analysts would, of course, fundamentally alter the DDO's standing with all non-CIA analysts as well.

The second Senate report, issued in February 1978, dealt with "The National Intelligence Estimates—A-B Team Episode Concerning Soviet Strategic Capability and Objectives." In mid-1976, at the suggestion of the now-defunct President's Foreign Intelligence Advisory Board, the DCI created a group of outside analysts, Team B, to engage in a "competitive analysis" with the insiders, Team A. It was not until after leaks to the press at the end of 1976, in which members of the B Team were characterized as "hawks" and those of the A Team as "doves," that the Senate Intelligence Committee took a special interest in the A-B Team experiment.

Its six-page report focuses not on the question of which team was right but rather on procedural issues and the tenor of the B Team. It does not explore why the two teams came up with divergent conclusions for National Intelligence Estimates (NIEs) and national security policy in general. Instead, the committee decried press leaks; noted that NIEs need improving; agreed that outside experts could be helpful; and voiced several truisms about the estimates process, including these: NIEs must meet the needs of policy-makers, competition and alternative analyses are to be encouraged, differences of judgment must be expressed, "strategic matters" should be better defined, and "policy-makers must define the questions not the answers."[34]

The third brief report of the Senate Committee, "The Soviet Oil Situation: An Evaluation of CIA Analyses of Soviet Oil Production," was issued in May 1977. In April 1977, President Carter had cited a CIA report on world energy during a news conference. DCI Turner later appeared before a House energy subcommittee and used additional data from the report. The *New York Times* then raised the question whether the CIA had "cooked" the facts in the report to fit Carter's recipe.

The committee studied the integrity of the intelligence process and the quality of the intelligence. The staff report found that the integrity of the process had not been compromised— that the study was made even before President Carter was inaugurated. It also found that the CIA had a good record and reputation for its analyses of Soviet oil production, that the estimates held up, that the CIA's open and classified sources were of good and unique quality, and that some of the classified data made a significant contribution to the study.

Early in 1979, the House Intelligence Subcommittee on Evaluation issued a brief report on U.S. intelligence performance *re* Iran prior to November 1978. It followed press reports of the President's dissatisfaction with the quality of political intelligence he had been receiving. The staff report attributed the failure to both the intelligence community and its consumers. The report asserts that intelligence collection and analysis were weak but also that intelligence did not challenge the policy-makers' confidence in the Shah, which in turn distorted the intelligence. Interestingly, the report did not consider whether the United States had the covert action capability to influence events in Iran, even if the requisite information had been available.

The report also pointed up the problems of collection in an area where there was no broad spectrum of contact with local groups and where U.S. relations and policy had become very closely tied to a single leader. The NIE process was found to be too cumbersome and not very useful to policy-makers in a fluid situation: the mechanics of the process tended to stifle dissent and suppress new ideas. Weak field reporting from all sources, according to the report, underestimated the strength and organization of the Shah's opposition, which simply confirmed the analysts' own complacency.

The Committees and the Media

It is no surprise that all four intelligence committees have tried to use or guide the media. Congressional leaders had to secure public support to succeed in restructuring U.S. intelligence. The case can be made that they have a positive responsibility to do so.

What is not wholly clear, however, is just *how* they have guided the media and in what precise *directions*. This is unfortunate. Were these methods and directions open to public scrutiny, it would be possible to make some adjustments for distortions that may have crept into the media coverage. But the relationships between the committees and the media remain murky.

The behavior of the Church Committee and its successor is somewhat easier to trace than that of its House counterpart. The Senate committees have been characterized by continuity, in part because they have had the same staff director and the same press spokesman. Clearly, the Church Committee had as its primary objective the public exposure of past wrongdoing to justify placing restrictions on the agencies and providing for closer oversight. The CIA, to be sure, was aware of its own transgressions well before the committee was created, and the DCI already had taken steps to prevent their recurrence. Indeed, because DCIs James Schlesinger and William Colby gathered together the so-called family jewels in one handy list, it was that much easier for some of the jewels to find their way into the *New York Times* and other publications. By June 1975, the public was well aware of many of the CIA's alleged transgressions when President Ford released the Rockefeller Report.

Presumably the Church Committee was intent on ensuring, through constant publicity leading ultimately to legislation, that these past abuses could never be repeated. Its leaders may also have hoped to uncover additional scandals and legal violations, but at the very least they wanted to build a foundation to justify tighter supervision.

For this reason, as press spokesman Spencer Davis has explained, the committee was quite open with the press.[35] Daily coverage of the committee's proceedings was encouraged, and the press was briefed on virtually all of the witnesses who appeared in closed as well as open sessions. During the first few months, when most of the hearings were closed, Sen. Church came before the cameras soon after each session. When the hearings were finally opened, almost all of them focused on past abuses. No public hearings were conducted on the problems of analysis and finished intelligence, clandestine collection, or matters of internal organization. Those that pertained to counterintelligence focused on possible violations of the law involving mail-openings and other forms of surveillance of Americans by Americans.

During this time, when both the public hearings and Sen. Church's press briefings were focused on past abuses, there was no close supervision of the staff's relations with the media. The staff was, of course, forbidden to disclose classified information (although Davis admits there were some leaks), and it was not supposed to discuss the committee's business with outsiders.

After the permanent Intelligence Committee was formed, however, a different press policy came into effect as the committee turned to current intelligence practices and activities. It is thus more acutely conscious, according to Davis, of its role in dealing with very sensitive matters affecting current sources and methods. Hence, relations with all outsiders have been more carefully controlled.

Only two staff members, Director Miller and Davis himself, are now authorized to discuss committee business with outsiders. Presumably they are to provide bona fide journalists and scholars with as much information as possible, consistent both with security and with freedom of information.[36]

It appears, however, that the committee has only slightly shifted its emphasis. It is still seeking to restrict the intelligence agencies along the lines of the Church report recommendations. This is clear from the amount of time it continues to devote to the rights of Americans, to oversight, and to budgets. It is clear also from the draft Charter and the committee's response to the hearings on it. The committee may be involving itself more with current intelligence matters and less with past abuses, but the evidence is far from clear. It should not be surprising, then, if media relations were also still following the old script.

Moreover, the committee's new rules are apparently being observed only fitfully. Certain themes appear to be pushed more than others, and certain "friendly" journalists still seem to have an inside track. This writer, also, has been present when members of various lobby groups were in communication with the staff, by telephone and on the scene, about committee work.

Perhaps some disregard of the rules is inevitable. Staff members have to seek information where they can find it, not only from government officials but also from journalists and knowledgeable outsiders. They also have to line up witnesses and prepare them for hearings.

What is not inevitable, however, is that the committee either deceive itself or maintain a public fiction. Senators both on and off the committee, journalists, and the general public should all be aware that private networks are active—involving, for example, some of the lobbies described in chapter 3, most of which have a particular (and very consistent) point of view about intelligence.

It is difficult to prove that the committee favors certain themes and journalists. Senior staff members claim that they are now more guarded with the press and that they do not play favorites. The real world, however, does not appear to be that simple.

One interesting example of the committee's relations with the press involves Joseph Trento of the *Wilmington News Journal*. Trento has a reputation in Washington for investigative reporting, and for dealing with controversial issues in a "controversial" way. In 1976, he became interested in the story of former U.S. ambassador to Chile Edward Korry. Korry had been highly critical of Sen. Church's 1973 investigation on the involvement of U.S. multinationals in Chile. Korry charged that Church's initial investigation was incomplete and that he had ignored, among other things, ITT's funding and its bribes of a number of Chilean politicians, including Allende himself before he became president. Korry also alleged that covert involvement by the U.S. government and private business with moderate democratic parties began at least as early as the Kennedy administration, and not with the Johnson-Nixon period as Church had maintained.

When Trento called the Church Committee to find out why they seemed to be ignoring the Korry reports, he himself was at first ignored. He was, of course, at that time an unknown journalist, working for a paper which did not carry the weight of better-known publications.[37] After he began publishing stories about Korry's account of events in Chile, however, he says he began to receive very different treatment. In December 1976 he was invited to meet with Spencer Davis. The meeting took place in a sound-proof cubicle in the committee's quarters.[38] (The committee occupies an old auditorium which has been partitioned into office space. This is not conducive to private discussion. Thus the committee had these special sound-proof cubicles built above the auditorium.)

According to Trento, Davis first asked him to turn off his tape recorder. He then offered to assist Trento with a story about the alleged involvement of the Copley News Service with the CIA, on the condition that Trento would stop pursuing the Korry matter. Trento says he refused.[39] Davis denies ever making such an offer.[40]

Trento, who also has broken several other major stories about intelligence, claims that this was not the only occasion when he was offered information in exchange for his cooperation. One of the senators on the committee, he alleges, also suggested to him that if he were more "polite" in his treatment of the committee's work, he would be likely to receive more help. Trento says he declined this offer as well: he maintains he has enough sources of his own to operate without special arrangements of this kind.[41]

The committee's alleged special relationships with journalists are not restricted to Trento, although no other comparable "arrangement" has surfaced to date. It is well known among some current and former staff members, for example, that certain journalists are more sympathetic than others. According to one former staff member, the more sympathetic, the better the treatment. Seymour Hersh of the *New York Times,* for example, was commonly referred to as "Uncle Sy" around the office and has been a frequent lunch companion of key staff members. Columnists William Safire and Robert Novak, who do not share Hersh's perspective, occupy a less favored category.

In this eminently public domain, private relationships sometimes predominate. In the past, the committee welcomed a certain kind of press coverage—one which emphasized agency abuses. Now the committee wants to justify its past concern, and to see it acted on. Quite naturally, it is partial to press coverage and journalists supportive of its view.

Natural enough, but—because Congress seeks both to reflect and to lead public opinion—unfortunate at the same time. It is difficult for the public to judge just how much the press is being "guided" and equally difficult for disinterested observers to evaluate the picture of intelligence which is being exposed to their view. Is it reliable? Or selective? Or significantly distorted?

The problem is exacerbated when the subject is sensitive, when hearings often are closed, and when information of any kind is scanty. It is even more troublesome when the rules specify that only two staff members may brief the press. Unless they are paragons, they could not possibly reflect equally the full spectrum of the committee's views.

There is no easy answer to this problem. Should the entire staff be muzzled, reserving to each committee member the exclusive right to provide information to the public? Conversely, should all members and all staff be let loose to say or do whatever each one might wish? Or should the press and public be excluded from the process, except for access to open hearings and published reports? There are advantages and disadvantages to any of these approaches. What does seem abundantly clear is that the present approach, ambiguous at best, serves the interests neither of Congress nor of the American people.

Conclusions

Congress, by any measure, is now playing a significant role in U.S. intelligence—of greater substance and depth, and with an intensity never before matched. It has reorganized its own procedures for continuing oversight. It has enacted major legislation and is considering more. It has released an unprecedented volume of information.

The legislative effort thus far appears to have had mixed results. Hughes-Ryan has increased congressional oversight. It also has made covert action a much more risky undertaking. The Foreign Intelligence Surveillance Act has increased the protection of American civil rights, but probably at some cost to effective counterintelligence and intelligence collection.

Up to now Congress has focused almost exclusively on publicizing past abuses and imposing restrictions to prevent their recurrence. It has paid scant attention to improving performance. It has examined the quality of analysis, judged it often to be poor, but it is not clear that substantial improvements have ensued. There has been one major series of public hearings on terrorism and some closed hearings on other aspects of intelligence. But there has been almost no congressional effort to evaluate our present capabilities in counterintelligence, covert action, and clandestine collection by human sources—and apparently none at all to improve them.

Missing also from the public record is evidence of any real attempt to assess future requirements. The permanent committees, of course, have been in operation for only a short time. But no congressional leaders have yet stepped out front, either to focus on the needs of the future or to suggest how Congress might begin coming to grips with building an effective intelligence capability. The very complexity of the subject combined with the absence of organized pressure groups concerned with improving intelligence and the paucity of academic centers for its study do not augur well for a serious and productive intelligence debate.

Congress also has made considerable strides toward continuing oversight and improving the protection of Americans from improper actions by their own government. Little has been done, however, to move on a parallel track to protect the American people from the more massive threats posed by both friendly and hostile foreign governments. This is no easy task—especially without revealing how much we know about such activities and how we came to know it. But the committees certainly have made less of an effort in this vital area than might reasonably be expected of them. Yet Congress still has the opportunity to shift its focus to the real intelligence needs of the future and the building of improved capabilities — and thus to enhance the quality of public understanding about the role of intelligence.

Congress might also consider serving in future as a vehicle for the dissemination of finished intelligence about developments around the world. For some time now, the executive has apparently been searching for an appropriate mechanism to provide the public with significant information of this kind. One obvious stumbling block is that even the most carefully sanitized analyses—drawing on declassified material only—might stir up diplomatic repercussions. And if the release and content of these analyses became domestic political footballs, the merit of the idea would be further compromised. Yet it has great potential. If a suitable mechanism can be devised, Congress may be able to play a role in national security policy formulation beyond its present anticipations.

CHAPTER THREE

The Role of Pressure Groups

ROY GODSON

THE "CLOSED WORLD" OF U.S. foreign intelligence is closed no more. Along with Congress and the press, public pressure groups have become significant participants in the debate about the shape and character of the intelligence establishment. These lobbies interact with Congress, the media, campuses throughout the United States, and even with the intelligence agencies themselves. They have become established actors on the Washington scene, and through grass-roots efforts, they have joined in the battle for public opinion nationwide.

By far the largest, best organized, and best financed are the groups that oppose major U.S. intelligence activities and seek major restrictions on the operation of the intelligence services. Their efforts took root in the late 1960s. In the late 1970s, they have become key players in Washington and around the country. They have helped draft important legislation. They have served as advisors and consultants to congressional committees, aiding in the selection of topics and witnesses for hearings. They have prepared, published, and distributed books, journals, periodicals, and films. They have serviced the press and scholars who request information and analysis and have provided speakers and materials for campus activities. They also have a grass-roots lobbying network which they bring into play when they believe it is needed.

The intelligence agencies are not entirely without supporters, however. Two small organizational efforts were begun in the mid-1970s by former senior intelligence officials. These organizations defend the scope and capabilities of U.S. intelligence more or less as it functioned in the 1950s and 1960s. They do not condone past abuses, but they have not devoted a significant part of their efforts to directly improving the quality of U.S. intelligence. Rather, they react and respond to the agencies' detractors: they do not initiate. Compared to "the opposition," their goals are limited and their resources lilliputian. They produce very little by way of books, journals, or periodicals and lack the staff and facilities to service Congress, the media, and the campuses in any systematic way.

This chapter describes the character, operations, and impact of these two groups. The more influential group may be referred to (for want of a better term) as the "anti-intelligence lobby." The organizations that make up this lobby are not necessarily opposed to all major aspects of U.S. intelligence, but they all believe that the clandestine services—those parts of U.S. intelligence engaging in clandestine collection, covert action, and counterintelligence—should be abolished and prohibited by law. The lobby is, however, divided on the question of tactics. Some of the more important groups seek to achieve their objectives by imposing legal restrictions on the agencies. Others attempt to destroy or weaken U.S. capabilities by more direct means—by the exposure of U.S. operations and methods and personnel. Nevertheless, in practice there is a great deal of cooperation among the groups and substantial evidence to indicate that the lobby has had significant impact, even if an assessment of its full effects is not yet possible.

The efforts of the two small groups of former professionals then will be considered. So far, the debate between the anti-intelligence lobby and the former professionals has been very limited. One side focuses on past abuses, whether alleged or real, and seeks to limit U.S. intelligence. The other side, adopting much the same agenda as its antagonist, also focuses on the past. No one has yet stepped forward to consider major reform in the context of specific future requirements. Thus the debate to this point has provided little insight into the obviously key question: What kinds of intelligence capabilities, processes, and methods are essential to satisfy these future requirements?

THE 'ANTI-INTELLIGENCE LOBBY'

The groups hostile to major aspects of U.S. intelligence represent a spectrum of opinion from the liberal to the radical left and from those who affirm the principal values of our society to those who frankly reject them. Yet they share a number of common characteristics. All of them are openly dedicated to the abolition of virtually all clandestine intelligence capabilities and operations. In public statements, conferences, books and congressional testimony, they maintain that *all* covert action and *almost* all secret intelligence collection should be abandoned. (Some of them apparently do not oppose technical means of collection, such as "spy satellites.") In effect, they want Congress to make it a crime for the United States to engage in on-the-ground espionage and covert action. They want to abolish clandestine human intelligence collection, counterintelligence, and covert action.

The chief rationale given for this position is couched in human rights terms. Its advocates claim that past and present U.S. intelligence activities have violated the rights of U.S. citizens at home, as well as the legitimate aspirations of peoples in the Third World. They maintain that the "unrestrained growth" of the intelligence agencies has created a "lawless state." As one characteristic study put it: "Using secret intelligence to defend a constitutional republic is akin to the ancient medical practice of employing leeches to take blood from feverish patients. The intent is therapeutic, but in the long run, the cure is more deadly than the disease."[1] Further,

> Secret intelligence agencies are designed to act routinely in ways that violate the laws or standards of society. As long as an overwhelming consensus exists on who the enemy is, few are troubled by the incompatibility. Over time, however, the secret activities of the intelligence agencies inevitably be-

come removed from the popular conception of what is necessary. Eventually, the society disagrees about the nature of the enemy. At that point, those who lead the dissent become a threat to the intelligence agencies, an enemy to the secret definition of national security.[2]

They also maintain that the intelligence agencies have sought to block legitimate aspirations for change in the Third World. As Richard Barnet, one of the founders of the lobby and a leading figure in the Institute for Policy Studies, put it ten years ago: "For more than twenty years the United States has carried on a global campaign against revolution and native insurgent movements, conducting a major military campaign or a C.I.A. operation in an underdeveloped country once every twenty months . . . . The United States has no alternative to offer the poor nations which is better than revolution, which, for all its brutality, has had some spectacular successes."[3]

Summarizing the themes of a major conference attacking covert operations a few years later, Barnet concluded:

> As long as the United States maintains its extravagant policy of trying to make the world safe for established political and economic power, there will always be men like Colby, Bissell and Hunt ready to lie, steal, and kill in that higher cause . . . . If we do not wish to use the state to legalize criminal activity at home and abroad, then we must stop trying to set the conditions for the internal development of other nations.[4]

Although there are some nuances among the anti-intelligence groups, they generally are opposed to all clandestine human intelligence collection as well as covert action. The American Civil Liberties Union told the Senate Intelligence Committee that all "clandestine collection abroad" should be prohibited in the absence of a congressional declaration of war. The rationale was this: (1)"no reasonable showing has been made to suggest that espionage in peacetime has more than a negligible value . . . . The questionable value of such activities must be balanced against many of the abuses and threats to the constitutional system. . ."; (2) espionage undermines "democratic freedoms and institutions abroad by improperly influencing the functioning of local media, political parties, unions, police forces, the military, and legislative bodies"; (3) espionage requires the maintenance of some "covert infrastructure" which carries the risk of running out of control and "about which the Church Committee expressed grave reservations"; (4) statutory authority for espionage diminishes "the moral and ethical standing of the United States in the world community"; and (5) untimely exposure of U.S. espionage can damage U.S. policy.[5]

Barnet argues that covert action and clandestine collection affect political conditions abroad, especially in "soft" or easily penetrable countries of the Third World. Both should be limited if not abolished completely—as instruments of U.S. policy, at any rate.[6]

The lobby apparently sees no danger to American civil rights or to Third World aspirations from the intelligence services of the Soviet Union and other "leftist" countries. It has expressed great concern about authoritarian governments in countries such as Chile, South Korea, and (until late 1978) Iran, and their intelligence services,[7] but it has virtually ignored the massive activities of the Soviet KGB (described to some extent in Appendix B) and those of services directly or indirectly allied with the KGB in Eastern Europe, Cuba, or other Communist countries.

This simply cannot be an oversight. The Soviet secret services are probably the largest in the world. Public information about KGB activities may be thin, but enough has been written that those concerned with wiretapping, surveillance, espionage, assassination, covert action, lying, blackmail, and the like cannot be wholly unaware of the danger they pose in and to the United States. Similarly, in its concern with progress and reform abroad, the anti-intelligence lobby presumably has made a determination that the Soviet Union and other Communist powers pose either a negligible threat to people in other countries or none at all.

A third characteristic of the groups which make up the lobby is a high degree of inter-organizational cooperation despite differences in tactics. The high degree of interaction among the major groups makes it difficult for an outsider to distinguish one from the other.

Legal Action Groups

Three principal anti-intelligence groups are made up primarily but not exclusively of lawyers: the National Lawyers Guild, the National Emergency Civil Liberties Committee, and the American Civil Liberties Union.

The *National Lawyers Guild* (NLG) was founded in 1936 as a professional organization for lawyers and soon fell under the control of Moscow-oriented Communists. After anti-Communist liberals such as Adolf Berle resigned from the NLG in 1940 and it was frequently cited by congressional committees as a "Communist Party front," its membership dwindled to a few hundred until it underwent a revitalization in the 1960s. Since then it has recruited a number of young lawyers and law students who look to the "revolutionary socialist society" of Castro's Cuba as their model. Under its current leadership, the NLG not only supported Cuba and North Vietnam but also has passed resolutions favorable to the Palestine Liberation Organization and other terrorist groups such as the Baader-Meinhoff gang in Germany. Nationwide, the guild has a budget of approximately $100,000 per year, a full-time staff of about ten, and at least double that number of volunteer lawyers and law students.[8]

In the late 1960s, the NLG started to provide legal services to activists seeking to avoid the draft, those charged with subversive activities in the military, and some individuals arrested in protests against U.S. involvement in the Vietnam war. The NLG also provided legal support for the Weatherman faction of Students for a Democratic Society and members of the Black Panthers who were accused of violent crimes. Several key NLG lawyers were involved in Daniel Ellsberg's defense in the Pentagon Papers case.

Pursuing these activities, the NLG became familiar with various forms of government surveillance, informants, and the use of grand juries to obtain information about radical and violence-prone groups. In 1972, it set up several projects specifically to explore limiting the use of grand juries and electronic surveillance. By the mid-1970s, the guild projects were expanded and came to involve senior staff members from both the Institute for Policy Studies and the American Civil Liberties Union.

The *National Emergency Civil Liberties Committee* (NECLC) was founded in the early 1950s, originally as the Emergency Civil Liberties Committee, to replace the Civil Rights Congress, which was more openly known for its ties to the Communist party U.S.A. Many of its leaders and active members are members also of the NLG and the ACLU. For example, from 1962 to 1968 its co-director was Henry M. diSuvero, who worked for the ACLU in New Jersey and then was elected president of the NLG in 1977.

The *American Civil Liberties Union* (ACLU) was founded in the 1920s as a socialist-pacifist organization which later expanded to become a watchdog on constitutional and civil rights. Since then, it has played a significant role on behalf of civil liberties and freedom of speech. Although it purged open Communists from positions of leadership in the 1940s, a number of leftist and radical lawyers and activists remained members. In the late 1960s, it became involved in the defense of anti-Vietnam protesters and dissenters.

Although some of its 250,000 members also were members and leaders of the more radical Emergency Civil Liberties Committee and the NLG, the ACLU was very cautious at first about working too closely with these other legal action organizations. After a gradual shift in the ACLU leadership in the late 1960s and early 1970s, however, the organization was drawn into anti-police surveillance work and its inhibitions about cooperation waned, so much so that many of its projects and personnel became all but indistinguishable from those of the other organizations. In 1971 the ACLU, making no distinction between domestic and foreign intelligence, declared that one of its top priorities was "the dissolution of the nation's vast surveillance network."[9]

To this end, the ACLU set up a "Political Surveillance" research project headed by Frank J. Donner, an old-time radical lawyer and NLG activist. Donner in 1975 became a member of the Advisory Board of *Counterspy* and a speaker for its successor organization, the Public Education Project on the Intelligence Community, which in 1977 became the Campaign to Stop Government Spying and is now known as the Campaign for Political Rights.

At the same time, the ACLU undertook to defend those seeking to publish classified information—John Marks and Victor Marchetti, for example—and instructed its Washington office to begin legislative action to end all political surveillance. In the mid-1970s, the ACLU and the Center for National Security Studies established a joint project in this connection, with the ACLU Foundation contributing at least $200,000 a year and several full-time lawyers to the effort.[10]

Other Organizations

The *Institute for Policy Studies* (IPS) was founded in 1963 by Marcus Raskin, Arthur Waskow, Gar Alperovitz, and Richard Barnet with the aim of "restructuring" American society. As an IPS report about its origin stated, the "government had become unresponsive and destructive in large part because all fresh political ideas and moral truths were smothered in the bureaucratic process," and "the universities were churning out false images and ideas because they insisted that social action be kept totally distinct from social theory except where it served the status quo."[11]

The institute was organized initially on an academic model, with resident, associate, and visiting "fellows." The fellows were assigned to develop projects and internship programs for college students. IPS still carries out such research efforts but with added emphasis on political action tactics aimed at Capitol Hill, the press, and the campus. Another operational pattern has emerged. The institute seeks additional funding for its projects and then encourages them to spin off as independent organizations.

In addition to institutionalizing its projects, IPS focuses a great deal of energy directly on Capitol Hill. It places interns in legislators' offices, invites members of Congress to participate in seminars, and enjoys considerable access to congressional offices. It also helped to initiate *Mother Jones* magazine and appears to have played a significant role in establishing the West Coast-based Pacific News Service in 1970. In late 1978, it also became the publisher of the biweekly publication *In These Times*.

As of mid-1979 IPS was operating out of its own five-story building in Washington, D.C. Its staff had grown from six to eight to twenty-five to thirty persons, and its annual budget of approximately a million dollars came mostly from the Samuel Rubin Foundation, with additional support from the Field Foundation and the Stern Fund.[12]

In the early 1970s, the institute, which since its founding has been critical of U.S. "intervention" abroad, began to focus directly on the intelligence agencies. A project on national security directed by Raskin, Robert Borosage, Richard Stavins, and George Pipkin, with a $20,000 grant from the Field Foundation, was established to conduct a broad survey of many aspects of intelligence, including corporate and private security programs. Borosage, Pipkin, and a number of other IPS staff members then formed the leadership of a spin-off, the Center for National Security Studies, and Raskin joined the advisory committee of *Counterspy*.

Stavins, an NLG attorney and IPS trustee, meanwhile directed an outgrowth of the national security project, the Project on Official Legality, which focused on assisting "national security whistle blowers" such as Daniel Ellsberg, Victor Marchetti, and Morton Halperin. In 1976, the project was expanded beyond the national security and intelligence agencies to include other branches of government and renamed the Government Accountability Project (GAP).

The *Organizing Committee for the Fifth Estate,* founded initially in 1972 as the Committee for Action/Research on the Intelligence Community, appears to have been formed by four very junior military intelligence officers who were active in Vietnam Veterans Against the War. In 1973 they published the first editions of a slim magazine, *Counterspy*.

By early 1974 the committee had merged with Norman Mailer's "Fifth Estate" project and obtained funding from the

DJB Foundation, established an advisory board, and assembled a new staff, including several lawyers and others active in the National Lawyers Guild. The new staff and advisory board (which also included IPS leader Marcus Raskin) made marked changes in the content and style of the publication. Articles in *Counterspy* now had much more research background, particularly about organized labor's alleged relations with the CIA, and listings of alleged CIA officers in U.S. embassies around the world. The organization also set up a student intern program, an Intelligence Documentation Center, and a grass-roots organizing effort including a speakers' bureau.

Nevertheless, the Organizing Committee remained very much a shoestring operation with a budget of around $14,000.[13] It maintained an irregular and tiny full-time staff and an erratic "quarterly" publication schedule.

Sometime during 1976, a number of the original staff departed, reportedly over internal dissent, leaving the organization in the hands of NLG activists, particularly William Schaap, Eda Gordon, Ellen Ray, and *Counterspy*'s lawyer, Alan Dranitske, who was also coordinator of the Cuba Subcommittee of the NLG's International Committee.

Philip Agee, former CIA operations officer, from his safe haven in Britain, continued to "name names" of alleged CIA personnel, but there were no major revelations in the United States for some time after what was claimed to be the last issue of *Counterspy* appeared in December 1976. Then in July 1978, Agee appeared with *Counterspy*'s Schaap and several others associated with the NLG at the Soviet-sponsored Eleventh World Festival of Youth and Students in Havana and announced the formation of Counter-watch. Schaap, also head of the Washington, D.C., NLG chapter, said the new group would develop a worldwide network of agents to expose CIA personnel and methods and would publish a new bimonthly magazine, *Covert Action Information Bulletin*.[14]

The *Center for National Security Studies* (CNSS) was launched in 1974 as an IPS spin-off with the stated intention of ensuring that national security "institutions do not become a permanent threat to the liberties and security they claim to protect."[15] The CNSS thus calls for an end to all covert operations and clandestine collection by human means—indeed, for the total dismantling of the clandestine services.[16]

At a major conference in September 1974, for which Senators Philip Hart (D-Mich.) and Edward Brooke (R-Mass.) were cohosts, the CNSS unveiled several ambitious research and action areas, among them:

1. *Project on Intelligence and Covert Action:* to encompass an extensive investigation of the activities and objectives of our intelligence institutions. (Soon thereafter this was renamed the Project on the Central Intelligence Agency, directed by John Marks.)

2. *Project on National Security and the Constitution:* to foster continuing debate on the proper scope of executive power in the area of national security. (This later became Morton Halperin's Project on National Security and Civil Liberties, jointly sponsored by the ACLU, which concentrates on the Freedom of Information Act and other litigation and lobbying for legislative restrictions on covert activities.)

3. *Citizens' Projects on National Security:* to work with a broad spectrum of citizens' groups to design forums in which national security issues can be placed before the public. (This project evolved in February 1977 into the Campaign to Stop Government Spying, which Halperin also headed until December 1978.)

According to a brochure designed to recruit college students for internships, the CNSS provides "information and expertise to concerned groups and individuals, the press and Congress . . . coordinating the efforts of citizens' groups and individuals about the issues . . . [and] developing reform proposals to hold national security institutions accountable to Congress and responsive to the people."[17]

The CNSS monitors national security issues related to intelligence and provides Congress and the executive branch with "expert testimony and technical assistance, analyzing how reform proposals can have loopholes which make things work differently in practice than in theory." As noted above, it works with the ACLU on litigation arising out of the Freedom of Information and Privacy acts. Its library serves as a resource for the press and scholars, and for the Campaign to Stop Government Spying. The CNSS issues a monthly publication, as well as books and monographs.[18]

Its staff ranges from six to ten full-time employees, and it operates on a budget of about $400,000 a year, most of which comes from the Field Foundation and the Veatch Program of the Unitarian Church.[19] Along with the Center for Defense Information, the Center for International Policy, and the "In the Public Service" media service, the CNSS is a project of the Fund for Peace, a private, non-profit, tax-exempt institution founded in 1967 "to promote greater knowledge and an understanding of the global problems that threaten human survival."[20]

The *Campaign for Political Rights:* this grass-roots organization appears to have had two parents—the Public Education Project on the Intelligence Community, an offshoot of *Counterspy,* and the CNSS Project on National Security, which in 1977 led to the National Conference on Government Spying, then to the formation of the Campaign to Stop Government Spying, which became, in late 1978, the Campaign for Political Rights.

The Campaign is a coalition of more than eighty religious, educational, and labor-related organizations from around the country, most of them small, "which have joined together to call for strict control on the operations of local, state, and national intelligence agencies."[21] It provides speakers, audiovisual materials, and printed materials for local use—its resources drawn usually from IPS, CNSS, NLG, ACLU, and *Counterspy* staff and alumni. Its four staff members in the Washington office have been associated with various of the other likeminded groups. Though small, the Campaign has contacts on campuses and with churches and the media in many parts of the country. Thus it provides one more route for bringing pressure to bear in Washington in support of objectives which are almost identical to those of the Center for National Security Studies.

As this run-down indicates, there is a high degree of cross-pollination among the groups within the anti-intelligence lobby. Leading figures move among the various organizations. They sit on one another's advisory boards, participate in one another's conferences, and write for one another's journals. Indeed, there is so much cross-citation of books and articles that, from the public's perspective, what may appear to be reinforcing arguments from many different sources comes down in the end to a single argument many times repeated.[22]

Two Tactical Approaches

The various groups within the lobby seem to differ most markedly on tactics. Clearly there are two major approaches. One, represented by the less radical elements such as the ACLU, concentrates on influencing legislation and congressional oversight, the internal rules and regulations of the executive branch, and moderate liberal opinion in academic, legal, and media circles. The other is far more radical in its professed goals and certainly in the ways it seeks to achieve them. Considering their similarity of views, it is hard to tell whether these tactical differences represent a conscious and coordinated division of labor, or whether they reflect pragmatic variations in skills, ideology, and sources of support.

The *moderate* group openly opposes all covert action and clandestine collection by human means and propagandizes widely for these objectives, using subtle tactics in dealing with Congress. It urges the adoption of legal restrictions on the intelligence agencies which would not prohibit covert action and clandestine collection outright but would make such operations difficult if not impossible. For example, they would prohibit the CIA from using various government agencies—the Peace Corps, the International Communications Agency, and AID —and various categories of non-governmental persons— journalists, clergymen, or academics—either as "cover" or as sources for agents. Even on the assumption that there ought to be reasonable limits on the agencies' uses of cover, such a blanket restriction would severely undermine their ability to function. The effect would be to deprive U.S. intelligence of valuable methods of operation and sources of information; it would, moreover, be far easier for foreign governments and terrorist groups to identify—and target—U.S. agents.

Similarly, legislating "criminal standard" restrictions on the surveillance of Americans and foreigners resident in the United States (as provided in the Foreign Intelligence Surveillance Act) imposes serious limits on positive U.S. collection and counterintelligence. There are clearly valid reasons to tighten up surveillance to avoid abuses. But by barring surveillance unless it can be proved in court that there is probable cause to believe a crime is about to be committed, the rather ironic effect is unilaterally to restrict U.S. intelligence operations while leaving foreign intelligence agents in this country to go freely about their business. After all, it is not "criminal" for any foreign intelligence service to set up "safe houses" or even to recruit informants in non-governmental U.S. organizations. A hostile foreign intelligence service, or a friendly one for that matter, is unlikely to obtain a judicial warrant to intercept electronic communications! Yet the anti-intelligence lobby, whatever the peculiarities of U.S. laws, maintains that past abuses of the "lawless state" require the enactment of restrictive legislation on U.S. intelligence.

It should be noted that many of the lobby's leaders are former intelligence officers, or former employees of State or Defense, and that they are quite knowledgeable about some classified matters. They are, however, careful to avoid being identified as the sources of leaks. Whatever their views about the practice, as a matter of policy they distance themselves from unauthorized disclosures in the media. As far as one can tell, such organizations as the CNSS, for example, have never divulged information which is not already in the public domain. Indeed, their reputation is such that they are consulted regularly by the congressional committees responsible for intelligence legislation and oversight, and some of their leaders are invited, and paid by the intelligence agencies themselves, to lecture on the pressing issues of the day.[23]

The tactical approach taken by the more openly *radical* groups—Counter-watch and *Counterspy,* to cite just two—

many of which profess sympathy with what they consider to be the "progressive" governments of the world such as Cuba and Vietnam, stands in sharp contrast to that of the moderates. These more radical groups appear to believe that the U.S. government is so tightly controlled by the military-industrial establishment that the more moderate efforts—legislation, regulation, and oversight—to restrict the intelligence services simply cannot work. Instead, they propagandize against U.S. intelligence in *all* forms and seek to render *all* of its operations difficult if not impossible to carry out. The clearest proponent of this tactic is former CIA officer Philip Agee. He is or has been at some time connected with *Counterspy* and *Covert Action,* the IPS, and some of the grass-roots organizations in the Campaign for Political Rights.

These groups have engaged in the deliberate disclosure of U.S. intelligence operations and personnel. The first to use such disclosure tactics as a major operational weapon were members of the North American Council on Latin America (NACLA), created in 1968, which seeks the support of those "who not only favor revolutionary change in Latin America but also take a revolutionary position toward their own society."[24] The NACLA was characterized in 1968 by a key leader of Students for a Democratic Society as the "intelligence gathering arm" of the New Left[25] and was credited by Agee in the British edition of his autobiographical *Inside the Company: CIA Diary,* along with members of the Cuban Communist party and the research facilities of the Cuban government, with having provided "vital research materials."[26]

Another organization credited by Agee and *Counterspy* with providing information leading to disclosures was a small, California-based research group, the Campaign for Democratic Freedoms. It apparently became "Research Associates International" and, later, "Transnational Feature Services." It specialized in reporting how democratic trade unions around the world were allegedly being manipulated by the CIA in behalf of U.S. business interests. This theme was later taken up by Agee and the staffs of *Counterspy* and *Covert Action* magazines.

But they go a good deal further than attempting to discredit the CIA for undermining democratic freedoms in the Third World. Agee and his colleagues try also to disrupt U.S. intelligence operations by publishing the names and addresses—and sometimes photographs—of U.S. intelligence officers working under U.S. embassy cover, and foreign nationals who allegedly are working for U.S. intelligence clandestinely, including secretaries and communications staff.[27] The exposure of secretaries and communications personnel can be especially pernicious. Operations may not be affected directly—these people work almost exclusively inside the embassies—but it adds to tension and anxiety, and thus to inefficiency, for those who have never been trained for hazardous duty. Nor are the results of disclosures always immediately apparent. Communications specialists, for example, may be particularly vulnerable; their mistakes can be enormously costly. Should they fail to encode their Washington transmissions properly, other governments can exploit such mistakes to break U.S. codes, with obvious and disastrous consequences for operations over a wide area.

In sum, whatever their tactical differences and the reasons for them, the anti-intelligence pressure groups compose a formidable lobby. In one decade they have managed to build a substantial infrastructure, mainly in Washington but also, through their grass-roots networks, with campus and media contacts all around the country. They generally maintain staffs with from twenty to twenty-five professionals, many of them very able lawyers and former U.S. national security officials. Their total operating budgets have been in the neighborhood of $800,000 a year.

A Significant Impact

With all the necessary caveats about precise measures of "influence," there is no question that the anti-intelligence lobby has had a significant impact. Several of the constituent groups have been deeply involved in legislative affairs and have directly and adversely affected intelligence capabilities.

A key indicator is their access to some of the most important people on Capitol Hill. When access is direct and continuous, and when congressional leaders and principal staff members are willing to devote time and attention to the views of particular groups, substantial influence is inevitable.

Beginning in the early 1970s, a number of younger former intelligence, State, and Defense Department officials—such as William Miller, Morton Halperin, John Marks, and Victor Marchetti—began to work with such IPS leaders as Richard Barnet and Marcus Raskin, who also were former government officials, with the objective of limiting U.S. intelligence operations. All of them were familiar, in varying degrees, with the workings of intelligence. Added to this core group were a number of lawyers whose organizations had provided legal support to the anti-Vietnam movement and who began in the early 1970s to focus their attention on government surveillance.

These former national security officials and lawyers recognized that if the powers of the U.S. intelligence agencies were to be curtailed, Congress would have to act. Congressional staffs were a key to their objective. Several of them took jobs as staff members and consultants and developed close ties with legislative leaders. The career of William G. Miller is a case in point. He left the U.S. foreign service in 1967 and became special assistant to Sen. John Sherman Cooper (R-Ky.) until Cooper's retirement in 1973. Miller then moved on to become staff director of the Senate Special Committee on National Emergencies and Delegated Powers, which was concerned with cutting back on the presidential powers which had accumulated during World War II, the Korean War, and the "cold war" generally. In this role Miller came to know Sen. Mike Mansfield, then Majority Leader, and Sen. Charles Mathias, both of whom promoted the work of the committee. They shared a belief that the Constitution was being undermined and abused as a result of uncontrolled activities by intelligence agencies,[28] and they were co-sponsors of a resolution calling for a special investigation which anticipated the establishment of the Church Committee.

In February 1975 Miller took over as staff director of that committee. At about the same time he became a consultant to the Center for International Policy, which, like the CNSS and several other organizations seeking radical alterations in U.S. national security policy, was sponsored by the Fund for Peace.[29] In May 1976 Miller became staff director of the permanent Senate Intelligence Committee, one of the principal arenas of the ongoing intelligence battle.

Morton Halperin took a different route. After resigning from Henry Kissinger's National Security Council staff in 1969, and later learning that he was a target of official wiretapping, he went to work for the Brookings Institution. He then secured a grant from a New York foundation and, in 1974, became "professional consultant" to the Senate subcommittee on intergovernmental relations which was concerned with legislative proposals to strengthen congressional oversight of the intelligence agencies. Several weeks before Seymour Hersh's articles in the *New York Times* (December 1974), this subcommittee, alleging massive CIA violations of its charter, considered the Mansfield-Mathias resolution to create a "Select Committee to Study Governmental Operations with Respect to Intelligence Activities." This committee was to be charged with conducting a two-year study of all the intelligence agencies and recommending any needed legislation to strengthen the congressional oversight role.[30] In January 1975, not long after the Hersh articles, the Senate did create such a committee—the Church Committee.

Halperin was among those who favored congressional investigations and oversight, as a starting point. Eighteen months earlier, for example, at a conference in New York, he explained to ACLU and other lawyers that these were but a prelude to limiting all covert action and clandestine collection.[31]

Halperin later became the associate director and then director of the Center for National Security Studies. He was an informal consultant to the Church Committee and now meets and corresponds regularly with key staff and members of Congress concerned with intelligence. Along with one or two ACLU lawyers, he is perhaps the most important lobbyist on these issues.[32]

John Marks, who was on the staff of the State Department's Bureau of Intelligence and Research in the late 1960s, became executive assistant to Sen. Clifford Case (R-N.J.) in 1970. During the next three years he concentrated on legislation to end the war and "to limit the intelligence community."[33] While still working for Senator Case, Marks joined with former CIA employee Victor Marchetti as co-author of *The CIA and the Cult of Intelligence,* which, after a court battle in which the ACLU took part, was published with some deletions in 1974. The book outlines much of the rationale for restricting the agencies which was adopted by the ACLU and the CNSS. Marks then joined the CNSS staff and became its associate director.

Access to Congress of this kind was nothing new to the leadership of the IPS. After leaving the national security bureaucracy, IPS co-founders Marcus Raskin and Arthur Waskow worked as congressional aides until they set up the institute. Although it describes itself as an "educational organization," the principal function of the IPS has always been to influence the influential, particularly on Capitol Hill. One of its early reports says:

> Because of its location in Washington and the associations of its Fellows with governmental officials, the Institute has been able to carry on a continuous, and constantly enriching, intellectual exchange with those in Congress and in the Executive Branch who frame public questions and implement policy.[34]

The IPS attracts literally dozens of congressmen and senators to its programs, and in 1964 it began to run seminars on "defense and disarmament" for members and their legislative assistants. The IPS also initiated an intern program which places "students" in congressional offices.

When the CNSS began operations in 1974, under the direction of NLG activist and IPS staff member Robert Borosage, it held a major conference castigating the CIA's clandestine operations; the conference was "hosted" by Senators Hart and Brooke in a hearing room of the Dirksen Senate Office Building, and CIA director William Colby participated in it. As a book based on the conference proceedings reported: "The dignity of the setting and the bi-partisanship of the hosts, as well as the recognized expertise of the participants, lent weight to the proceedings and papers."[35]

American Civil Liberties Union officials have testified at most hearings on major legislation, from FISA to the draft Charter. Its lawyers coordinate key projects with the CNSS and meet frequently with congressional leaders and senior staff, as well as White House officials who are concerned with intelligence.[36]

Why, then, do groups like the ACLU and the CNSS enjoy such access to Congress? There seem to be four reasons: they are highly knowledgeable; they have a ready "reform" agenda; they are able to mobilize impressive constituencies; and they fit into the current mood in official Washington.

Expertise. These groups *are* knowledgeable. They provide legislators and their staff with a pool of expertise which is usually free of charge. A number of senior staff members who often are in contact with the CNSS, for example, explained in interviews that, outside of the intelligence agencies themselves, there are few people who can give them insights into the complex mysteries of clandestine intelligence. The committees hire former intelligence professionals to assist them, and some of these consultants are mild critics of covert operations and clandestine collection. Some committee members still want advice from able and knowledgeable "outsiders"—genuine outsiders—who are interested in thoroughgoing reforms rather than technical adjustments.

The reform agenda. The lobby groups have the field largely to themselves. A congressional consensus has developed that *something* must be done. Former high-ranking intelligence officials do meet occasionally with the staffs, and they testify and lobby from a "pro-intelligence" perspective. But with only a few exceptions, they are not interested in major reforms. While they may be willing to contemplate some modest degree of additional oversight, they do not believe that Congress or the public can much improve U.S. intelligence capabilities—indeed, they think it would be most helpful if the intelligence profession were left to the professionals. They may well be right. But so far the only groups ready and willing to weigh in on the side of greater congressional involvement have been those in the anti-intelligence lobby.

Mobilizing support. While these groups may not be able to influence many voters or win many elections, they can pull together a substantial nationwide constituency. Morton Halperin told this writer that they are able to mobilize a wide spectrum of groups and centers of influence—"from pickets in Indiana to the editorial board of the *New York Times.*" He went on to say that the extremes of this coalition are not always easy to control (e.g., the more radical elements that seek direct confrontation) and that the leading newspapers do not always see eye to eye with the CNSS. Nevertheless, because the anti-intelligence lobby can mobilize campus activists as well as such leading liberal organizations as Americans for Democratic Action and the ACLU, and because it has access to key media people, it does wield significant influence. In the debates which led to the passage of major legislation—S.Res. 400, for example, which established the permanent Senate Intelligence Committee, and the Foreign Intelligence Surveillance Act—both the Republicans and the Democrats argued that if a coalition spanning the ACLU and the intelligence agencies themselves could agree on something, then surely it must be a good thing. When such a coalition has formed on any particular issue, it has usually ensured relatively smooth sailing. Opposing views tend to be defused in advance.

Reflecting the temper of the times. The anti-intelligence pressure groups also exert influence because they appear to reflect the pervasive mood of Congress (or what has been its mood for the last five years). Since the late 1960s a consensus has emerged supporting closer scrutiny and stronger control of the agencies. To some extent, indeed, the intelligence "issue" has been depoliticized. There was relatively little partisan dissension in the aftermath of the Church Committee report. Both Senate liberals and conservatives supported the creation of a permanent committee, and the Foreign Intelligence Surveillance Act passed by a 95-1 vote. Nor has there been much overt partisanship within the intelligence committees. The staff apparently works largely as a unit. Even committee members who have been critical of much of the drift of congressional action have co-sponsored a draft Charter in an effort at least to get the discussion started, although this draft legislation seeks to impose severe restrictions on covert action and clandestine collection and provides little or nothing in the way of improved quality and performance. There has been considerably more dissension in the House, particularly from conservatives.

Simultaneously, the CIA and the FBI, demoralized by persistent attacks and the exposure of the "family jewels," and by the departures and forced resignations of many senior officials in the clandestine services, may well have been looking for any reasonable shelter in the storm. Rather than go on the offense and seek a return to the *status quo ante* regarding restrictions and oversight, or try to persuade Congress to focus instead on repairing the agencies' defects and building their capabilities, they were apparently prepared to settle for the easy way out. The effect has been to let the intelligence committees and the major groups in the "anti" lobby set the terms of the debate.

There has been considerable disagreement about the impact of the lobby. Some members of the House and Senate and key staff vigorously denied in interviews that the lobby played a major role in their deliberations. In one sharp exchange in the hearings record, several senators expressed outrage at the suggestion they had been influenced by pressure groups at all.[37] Others, however, on both sides of the debate, have acknowledged the significant influence of such groups. Sen. Edward Kennedy (D-Mass.), while leading the fight for FISA on the Senate floor, singled out the ACLU for its "excellent work."[38] Rep. Jim Wright (D-Tex.) pointed with favor to the fact that the ACLU was in agreement with Presidents Ford and Carter and the leaders of the FBI, CIA, and NSA, and said that "the ACLU has [had] tremendous input insofar as this legislation is concerned."[39] Rep. Robert Kastenmeier (D-Wisc.) argued in the debate on the Conference Committee report on FISA that "we have developed a unique historical consensus— supported by everyone from the FBI and CIA to the ACLU. I believe it is imperative that this consensus not be allowed to disintegrate at this late hour."[40]

Certainly the groups themselves believe that, within limits, they have been influential. They point out that even before

Congress began to move on intelligence issues in the mid-1970s, they had already defined the agenda for congressional action. Their proposals to investigate the agencies and set up permanent oversight processes have been accomplished. The Foreign Intelligence Surveillance Act by and large reflected their views, although they would have preferred to go much further. The draft Charter, S.2525, also coincides with their thinking—even though it does not, as they would prefer, abolish all espionage and all covert action. Although the anti-intelligence lobby can never get too far out in front of Congress, it has in fact helped greatly to determine the general direction—and possibly to push Congress further than it might otherwise have gone.

The lobby's second major approach—that of propaganda and disclosures—has also had some effect. Disclosure tactics began as early as 1967, when *Ramparts* magazine and one prominent former CIA official, Tom Braden, alleged that certain student and labor organizations had received CIA funding. But this was viewed as an aberration. Similarly, when a book published in East Germany in 1968, *Who's Who in the CIA*, listed Hubert Humphrey and Eugene McCarthy along with the names of some real agents, it was dismissed as crude Soviet propaganda.

The current stream of disclosures dates from 1973 and 1974, when research reports of the NACLA and the Campaign for Democracy started to appear in *Counterspy*. The names and projects listed in this magazine and in Agee's *Inside the Company* (1975), which were picked up and reprinted in various newspapers and journals, including scholarly ones,[41] could not as readily be dismissed as aberrations or as pure, unadulterated, Soviet-inspired disinformation—although nor could many be verified. Moreover, when all of this material was supplemented by congressional leaks—about Chile, and covert U.S. support of the Kurds and of Italian political parties—and the listing of code names and even real names in the Church Committee investigations, there were those both here and abroad who began to wonder if anything could be kept secret in the United States.[42]

The stream of disclosures has continued. This may not have crippled clandestine collection altogether, but it does appear that U.S. capabilities have been damaged in some places. A number of former and current senior U.S. intelligence officials point out that both American and foreign individuals, as well as foreign intelligence services, no longer believe that they can trust the U.S. services to maintain confidentiality. There is still cooperation, of course, but reportedly they no longer are supplying the quality of information for analysis and counterintelligence which they used to provide. How much they are holding back it is impossible to say.[43]

Covert action also appears to have been weakened. It is particularly difficult to assess the damage in this area because the United States had dramatically reduced covert operations even before the spate of disclosures in the mid-1970s. Clearly, however, the damage to U.S. capabilities has been real: covert action is now more expensive and more risky, and a longer leadtime is required to recruit personnel. Policy-makers can probably still engage in political activities abroad which do not show the U.S. hand, but this option is certainly less attractive than before.

By the same token, the morale of U.S. intelligence personnel has surely been shaken. This is difficult to measure but nonetheless real—involving personal anxiety and tension, increased risks of violence, and the potential of harassment by political extremists, all of which may contribute to operational errors by people under severe stress.[44]

EFFORTS OF FORMER INTELLIGENCE PROFESSIONALS

In contrast to the long-term, well-calculated, well-financed, and well-organized efforts of the anti-intelligence lobby, there is relatively little to report about the activities of "the other side." Assuming that there are no major organizations or networks in operation other than those which have come to public attention, there would appear to be one quite small organization of former intelligence officers and one very small unit within a larger multipurpose organization, plus a few individuals, who have become involved in the U.S. intelligence debate.

Their professional experience gives them some advantages, of course. But also it somewhat ironically limits their effectiveness. For one thing, they are acutely conscious of the sensitive information which they possess and which might inadvertently be revealed in the heat of public debate. Then, too, they are not regarded as disinterested participants. Many of them have been at the center of the dramas, investigations, and revelations of the last few years. Their expertise is unquestioned, but they are simply not perceived to be "impartial" students and observers of the subject of intelligence.

More than anything else, however, they limit themselves: they tend to be defensive and reflexively pro-intelligence, hence limiting further their effectiveness. They have been concerned mainly with defending the agencies from the assaults of the anti-intelligence lobby and what they feel are the distortions of the congressional investigations and the media coverage. They have not attempted to defend every past practice; indeed, to some extent they have supported legislative efforts to control the agencies' activities more closely. But they have been unwilling to address critically the major intelligence weaknesses of the past or to make specific proposals to meet the needs of the future. They have, as a consequence, tended to adopt the "enemy's" agenda.

The *Association of Former Intelligence Officers* (AFIO) is the most active and, up to now, the most important organization within the "pro-intelligence" forces. Lobby may be too strong a term in this instance. The group was founded in May 1975 by a few ex-CIA officers as the Association of Retired Intelligence Officers. In 1976 it opened its membership to professionals from other intelligence agencies and changed its name slightly. It now has about 2,800 dues-paying members, a little over half of whom had worked primarily in military intelligence.[45]

The leadership and some 150 active members reflect a variety of views about intelligence and other political issues. What unites them all is the belief that the public has been given a seriously distorted understanding of intelligence and has had little opportunity to get accurate information. The AFIO has stepped into the vacuum to defend the intelligence services from the more extreme attacks and to put the subject into better perspective for public debate. They do not, however, see their mission as critiquing, revamping, or reforming U.S. intelligence services, which they believe functioned effectively before the attacks of the early 1970s and would function equally well today if permitted to do so.

The AFIO's resources are severely limited. It relies largely on voluntary assistance; its small treasury, derived solely from dues and small donations, has been used to hire an executive director and a part-time secretary/administrative assistant. The AFIO rents a small office in McLean, Virginia—all on a budget of about $25,000 a year.

Its principal activities are public relations and education. When asked, it has given testimony at congressional hearings. The AFIO has responded to about 500 requests for speakers from high schools and colleges and from the media; it has provided its membership around the country with a speakers' kit; it publishes a bimonthly newsletter, *Periscope,* which provides some information on the intelligence debate; and it has assisted a number of authors and scholars in preparing books and articles on intelligence-related subjects. It also monitors the media and attempts to get its viewpoint into print and on television.

The AFIO has been consulted by most of the relevant committees and has provided private briefings and, up to now, the only systematic public critiques of the draft Charter and the Foreign Intelligence Surveillance Act. It encourages its members to express their views directly to Congress and its committees.

As a rule, the AFIO refrains from public criticisms of past and present intelligence practices. It did question CIA director Stansfield Turner about his reductions in clandestine services personnel and what it thought might be a growing deemphasis on intelligence collection from human sources; it then apparently accepted the agency's explanations, although some specialists in a position to know did not.[46] When the CIA apparently allowed a situation to develop in which a very junior employee, William Kampiles, was able to steal the top-secret KH11 Manual from the operations center, the AFIO remained silent; a former senior agency official (who also is an AFIO member), however, pointed out that this sort of serious breach of security should have been avoided by the agency itself.[47] The AFIO's persistent disinclination to engage in any specific criticism at all of the way the agencies conduct the business of intelligence has until now left the debate and the impetus for reform in the hands of those who favor radical change.

Up to now, the AFIO has mounted the only sustained non-governmental effort to re-establish the credibility of clandestine intelligence. But it has not been able to amass sufficient funds or mobilize its potential constituency—which numbers probably in excess of 50,000 former intelligence professionals—to achieve even its limited goals. While it is beginning to cast about for additional sources of support, to become something more than a volunteer organization of some very able and experienced professionals operating on a shoestring, it is not likely in the foreseeable future to be able to match the resources of the anti-intelligence lobby.

In spite of some efforts to collaborate with other organizations of former intelligence officers—the Central Intelligence Retiree Association and the National Counter-Intelligence Corps Association, for example, which have been almost exclusively social—it seems doubtful that any activist umbrella organization of former intelligence professionals will emerge to mobilize what potentially could be a potent lobby. Already there is another competing organization. Further, some members of the AFIO are critical of what they see as an overemphasis on public relations and would prefer instead to focus on the specific needs of the future. Then, too, many former professionals do not wish to join any public organization and do not believe in public education about what they point out is and ought to remain essentially a non-public matter.

The *Security and Intelligence Fund* was formed in 1978 under the auspices of the American Security Council, a "pro-defense" organization headquartered in Washington, D.C., and Boston, Virginia. The Security and Intelligence Fund is headed by James Angleton, former CIA counterintelligence chief, and a number of other former high-ranking national security officials. Its stated purpose is to "stop the intelligence wrecking crews and to revitalize the decaying intelligence and counterintelligence capabilities"[48] of the United States.

Although the organization sends out an occasional Situation Report and has contributed over $10,000 to the Special Agents' Legal Fund—to help defray the expenses of former FBI officials indicted for alleged improprieties in their pursuit of the Weatherman fugitives—it has focused almost all of its attention on Capitol Hill. A direct-mail fund-raising appeal stated, "To help defeat the measures that threaten to dismantle our intelligence community your Fund has employed a full time Congressional relations expert," and again, "At this stage, our resources and our time are being concentrated on the task of keeping these left wingers in Congress from emasculating our national intelligence services."[49] While the fund lobbied against the Foreign Intelligence Surveillance Act and provided a fact-sheet on the draft Charter, its lone staff member apparently has not established a major presence on the Hill.

In addition to these two small organizations, a number of former high-ranking government officials and senior intelligence officers have been active in their own right. Former cabinet members and senior officials with broad national security interests—Robert Bork, William Simon, and Clare Boothe Luce, for example, and former CIA directors Helms, Colby, and George Bush—have taken some part in the public debate; some of them have testified and lobbied against tight restrictions on the intelligence agencies, and some have helped generate financial and moral support for the indicted FBI agents.

It is difficult to estimate the extent of this activity, much less measure its effect. But in any case these individual efforts, like those of the organizations discussed above, generally have been defensive. They have been geared to limiting the damage to U.S. intelligence and have not been aimed directly at finding new ways of improving U.S. capabilities and performance.

The small organizational efforts, coupled with those of individuals, do act as something of a counterweight to the anti-intelligence lobby, but they clearly are outmatched in terms of both staff and resources.

Even more important, however, so far they have not become involved in formulating strategies and proposals to guide the future. In the midst of a national debate about the reshaping of the intelligence services, and with Congress and essentially hostile pressure groups deeply engaged, there are no competing pressure groups. Thus, even if the option to engage in covert action, clandestine collection, and counterintelligence is preserved for the United States—and this battle is by no means settled—the opportunity for non-governmental organizations to work with Congress and the President to ensure that this country has first-class intelligence capabilities to meet the needs of the future may be lost.

CHAPTER FOUR

The Performance of TV Evening News

ERNEST W. LEFEVER

AT THE END OF World War II, the most influential media of public information and debate were newspapers, magazines, and the radio. But by the early 1970s television appeared "to have taken over as America's prime source of current information," according to a comprehensive study whose findings have been confirmed by virtually all other authoritative research.[1] According to polls, the majority of young persons and adults, including the college educated, rely more on TV than on any other source for their knowledge of current affairs, and trust it more.

The influence of TV news on public debate complements that of the printed press, especially the *New York Times,* usually regarded as the national newspaper of record. The *Times* is addressed to America's elite. Its primary audience includes top leaders in the policy-making community in Washington and in the national communications media, particularly in the news departments of the three commercial TV networks. The impact of the *Times* tends to impose a stamp of sameness on TV news departments, which rely on it heavily in defining what the news

---

NOTE: Gregory B. Conover, a graduate student at Georgetown University, was responsible for gathering, tabulating, and analyzing the statistical data from the Vanderbilt Television News Archives on which much of this chapter is based.

is and which stories should be given greatest play. Edward Jay Epstein and other media analysts have pointed out that TV news executives and editors tend to be exposed to similar information and a similar interpretation of events because of their reliance on the *Times*. He quotes one executive: "Like it or not, the *Times* is our bible; it tells us what is likely to be considered important by others."[2]

Television's dramatic and vivid combination of news and views has a powerful, it not precisely measurable, impact on the attitudes and behavior of millions of citizen-viewers, including members of Congress and of the executive branch. The communication, however, is not all one way. Policy-makers attempt to turn TV news to their own uses and in some measure succeed in doing so. Public figures who have access to thirty or sixty precious seconds on the evening news of ABC, CBS, or NBC—and especially all three, repeatedly—possess a powerful weapon of influence in our media-saturated society. All sides in the recent debate over foreign intelligence have attempted to use this weapon, with mixed results.

As a broadcast medium whose channels are licensed by the federal government, TV, like radio, is legally obligated to serve "the public interest" and abide by the Fairness Doctrine in its presentation of all public issues. This doctrine is rooted in "the paramount right of the public in a free society to be informed and to have presented to it for acceptance or rejection the different" viewpoints on "controversial issues."[3] The Fairness Doctrine has the force of law and has been upheld by the Supreme Court.[4] It is designed to encourage "robust debate." To achieve this, the broadcaster is required to provide accurate news in a meaningful context and has an "affirmative duty" to seek out spokesmen for contrasting opinions and perspectives. When presenting opposing views, the broadcaster must provide "a reasonable opportunity" for each to be heard. Any radio or TV station—and by implication a network—has a right to advocate particular views, but it has a corresponding obligation to present contrasting opinions.

While the Fairness Doctrine applies to a station's or network's total public-affairs programming (news, documentaries, and panel shows), the ABC, CBS, and NBC evening news programs with their vast audience and influence have a special obligation to observe the spirit of balance and fair play implicit in the doctrine. It is against this standard that the evening news shows of the three commercial TV networks will be measured in this chapter, with special reference to their "affirmative duty" to seek out spokesmen for opposing views and to present facts that lend perspective to the events being reported.

Patterns and Themes in TV News

This survey covers the evening news programs of the three TV networks from January 1974 through October 1978, a period of intensive media and public interest in the CIA. In September 1974, a memorandum by Rep. Michael Harrington (D.-Mass.) revealing secret activities of the CIA in Chile made its way into the press, and in December of that year Seymour Hersh started his series of *New York Times* articles critical of the CIA, particularly of its role in monitoring the behavior of certain U.S. citizens. From then to the present, the congressional committees probing real or alleged abuses by the CIA, and seeking to enact legislation to prevent further misdeeds, have assiduously used the media to advance their causes.

Each of the three evening news programs broadcasts an average of 22.6 minutes of news and interpretation every weekday. Some Saturday and Sunday evening network news is included in this survey, and with this each network averaged 103.9 hours a year. These programs have a combined audience of about 40 million households for 275.9 days a year. This gives the TV newsmen a "bully pulpit" of which Theodore Roosevelt could scarcely have dreamed.

This study of TV coverage of intelligence is drawn from the monthly *Television News Index and Abstracts* published by the Vanderbilt Television News Archives in Nashville, Tennessee, the most respected and reliable source for such information. These monthly publications carry a detailed index of about thirty three-column pages and an accurate summary of all news items on each TV network evening news program. The exact duration of each story is given along with the names of the newsmakers and newscasters. We did not use the videotapes or full transcripts because experience has shown that the additional time and expense required to cover such a long period would not yield significantly different results. (In a previous study I headed a team that analyzed how CBS-TV evening news presented U.S. foreign and defense issues in 1972 and 1973.[5] We consulted the full transcripts for 1972 and the Vanderbilt *Abstracts* for 1973. In certain cases we compared the videotape with the abstract and concluded that the margin of error always present in content analysis was not appreciably increased if one examined only the abstracts. The abstract appeared to be an accurate reflection of both the substance and the mood of the full transcript of any particular news story or comment.)

The first step in the present study was to identify all TV evening news stories bearing on U.S. and foreign intelligence between January 1, 1974, and October 31, 1978. (The monthly *Abstracts* for the last two months of 1978 had not yet been published when the tabulation was made.) By consulting the extensive index of each *Abstract,* we developed a list of twenty key topics directly related to intelligence:

1. Information leaks
2. Chile
3. Angola
4. Domestic surveillance
5. U.S. covert operations abroad
6. Assassinations in the United States
7. Assassinations abroad
8. Foreign espionage in the United States
9. Watergate
10. Investigations
11. Personnel and administration
12. Reforms and reorganization
13. Drug tests
14. Energy estimates
15. Poison stockpiles
16. Use of journalists
17. Submarine recovery

18. Presidential candidate briefings
19. Foreign espionage outside the United States
20. Reports on foreign situations

The overwhelming majority of these topics dealt with the CIA. Within the two foreign espionage topics (8 and 19), 90.78 per cent of the coverage dealt with Soviet-bloc intelligence activities, followed by 5.06 per cent for the Korean CIA, 3.70 per cent for the Chilean Secret Service, 0.27 per cent for Egyptian intelligence, and 0.18 per cent for Communist China. Brief and incidental references to intelligence agencies of other states, such as those to SAVAK's activities within Iran in stories about Iranian student protests in the United States, were not included in the study.

Virtually every news story, whether on CIA leaks or on intelligence activity at home or abroad, carried one or more themes. A theme may be defined as a recurring idea or judgment, a persistent perspective or attitude toward a topic. For example, CIA activity in Chile is a subject, the view that the CIA in Chile acted illegally or immorally is a theme. In our study we identified nine major themes in stories about the CIA:

1. Engages in immoral or illegal activities
2. Is not sufficiently accountable
3. Engages in questionable activities
4. Is corrupt or untrustworthy
5. Is incompetent or ineffective
6. Is endangered by excessive publicity, criticism, and political influence
7. Performs essential intelligence functions
8. Is effective and accountable
9. Seeks to maintain necessary secrecy

The first five themes are critical of the CIA, whether or not the particular criticism is justified, while the last four embrace a positive appraisal of the CIA, again whether justified or not.

In the following pages we will first tabulate the time given to each of the twenty subjects by year and TV network. This will establish the *pattern* of TV coverage of U.S. intelligence. Then we will note the time given to each theme, again by year and network. This will indicate the *flow* of TV's treatment of the intelligence story. We will conclude with an analysis of subjects and themes—both favorable and unfavorable—and what this says about the role of commercial television's evening news in the debate over U.S. foreign intelligence during the past five years. We will also make some observations on the contribution TV has made to the public's understanding of KGB activities in the United States and abroad.

TV News on Intelligence by Subject

Reports on U.S. and foreign intelligence activities occupied a very small part of the available 22.6 minutes of each of the three evening news shows from 1974 through 1978. In 1975, when the topic was most active, the network providing the most coverage, CBS, gave only 5.14 per cent of its broadcast time to this topic. The distribution is given in table 2.

The fourfold upsurge of TV attention to intelligence news from 1974 to 1975, shown in table 1, was occasioned largely by the unauthorized disclosure of Rep. Harrington's memorandum on CIA activity in Chile, Seymour Hersh's "exposure" of the CIA's "domestic spying" in the United States, and the establishment early in 1975 of select committees in both the House and the Senate to investigate American intelligence agencies. As the table shows, there were no significant differences among the networks in the volume of attention given to intelligence.

The year-by-year analysis by subject of all three networks combined gives a much more precise picture of the topics the evening news focused on. In the following five tables, 3 through 7, each news item, as defined by the Vanderbilt Television News Archive, was placed in only one intelligence category, with a few exceptions that were divided in the interest of accuracy. In every case, the news item was listed under the most specific subject. The length of each report in minutes and seconds was provided by the Vanderbilt *Abstracts*.

In 1974 (table 3), overwhelming attention was given to the CIA—93.33 per cent, compared with 6.67 per cent for foreign espionage abroad and in the United States. The four top stories, each dealing largely with alleged misdeeds of the CIA,

TABLE 2

TV Evening News Devoted to U.S. and Foreign Intelligence: 1974–1978
(As a percentage of total time, by year and network)

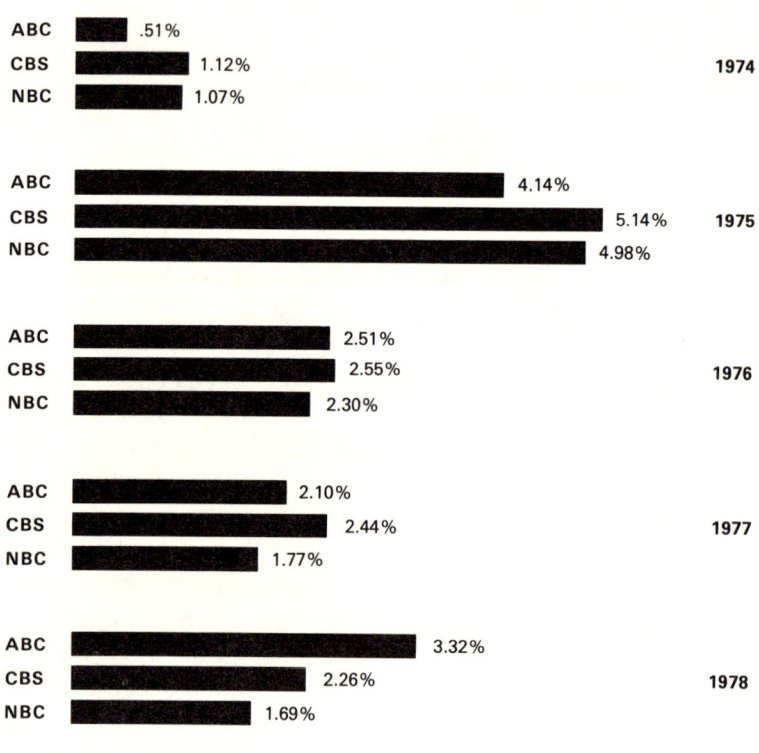

made up 79.3 per cent of the total intelligence news. Allegations of CIA "destabilizing" operations in Chile led the list, followed by revelations of the monitoring of American citizens in the United States. CIA involvement in Watergate came third, and CIA covert operations abroad (other than in Chile) fourth.

In 1975 (table 4), stories on domestic spying and foreign assassinations by the CIA made up 40.34 per cent of the total

TABLE 3

U.S. AND FOREIGN INTELLIGENCE TV NEWS: 1974
(ABC, CBS, and NBC Evening News Combined)

During 1974 there were 812 TV evening news programs averaging 22.59 minutes of news each. The three networks carried 92 news items on U.S. and foreign intelligence. They are tabulated below by subject, with the total number of minutes given to each and its percentage of the total intelligence news.

Subject	Minutes	Percentage of Total
1. Chile	43.33	25.87
2. Domestic Spying	37.33	22.27
3. Watergate	34.83	20.79
4. U.S. Covert Operations Abroad	17.33	10.35
*5. Foreign Espionage Outside U.S.	10.67	6.37
6. Reforms and Reorganization	6.83	4.08
7. Foreign Assassinations	4.67	2.79
8. Personnel and Administration	4.50	2.69
9. Information Leaks	2.67	1.59
10. Energy Estimates	2.50	1.49
11. Reports on Foreign Situations	2.33	1.39
*12. Foreign Espionage in U.S.	.50	.30
Total	**167.50**	

* Indicates subjects related to foreign intelligence agencies totaling 11.17 minutes or 3.98%. All other subjects are related to the CIA.

TABLE 4

U.S. and Foreign Intelligence TV News: 1975
(ABC, CBS, and NBC Evening News Combined)

During 1975 there were 842 TV evening news programs averaging 22.58 minutes of news each. The three networks carried 476 news items on U.S. and foreign intelligence. They are tabulated below by subject, with the total number of minutes given to each and its percentage of the total intelligence news.

Subject	Minutes	Percentage of Total
1. Domestic Spying	205.83	22.74
2. Foreign Assassinations	159.33	17.60
3. Personnel and Administration	129.50	14.31
4. Investigations	102.67	11.35
5. U.S. Covert Operations Abroad	58.00	6.41
6. Angola	47.00	5.19
7. Chile	38.67	4.27
8. Submarine Recovery	37.83	4.18
9. Domestic Assassinations	29.83	3.30
10. Poison Stockpile	24.83	2.74
11. Drug Tests	19.83	2.19
12. Information Leaks	13.17	1.45
13. Watergate	12.00	1.33
*14. Foreign Espionage in U.S.	9.50	1.05
15. Reforms and Reorganization	6.67	.74
16. Reports on Foreign Situations	5.00	.55
17. Use of Journalists	3.50	.39
*18. Foreign Espionage Outside U.S.	2.00	.21

Total 905.17

*Indicates subjects related to foreign intelligence agencies, totaling 11.5 minutes or 1.27%. All other subjects are related to the CIA.

intelligence news on evening programs. As in 1974, Communist espionage here and abroad received almost no attention, 1.27 per cent of the total. In January 1975, President Ford appointed a commission under the chairmanship of Nelson Rockefeller to investigate U.S. foreign intelligence. Its report was published in June.[6] Although it acknowledged the necessity for U.S. intelligence and generally spoke well of CIA activities, it referred to CIA abuses—opening of U.S. mail, infiltration of other agencies, a Mafia connection, and support of attempts to assassinate Castro. All this fueled stories in the media. In December 1975, Richard Welsh, the CIA station chief in Athens, was murdered after his name and identity had been published in *Counterspy*, an anti-CIA newsletter, though no direct cause-and-effect relation has been established.

In February 1976 (table 5), President Ford issued Executive Order 11905 designed to reorganize the intelligence community. Congress was also very active that year, establishing a new Senate Intelligence Committee in May and publishing in July the first report of its earlier investigative committee chaired by Sen. Frank Church (D.-Idaho). Not surprisingly, the top two stories totaling 28.35 per cent focused on the administration, reform, and reorganization of the intelligence community. Interest in the CIA's covert operations remained high, with the focus shifting from Angola to Chile. The networks gave only 3.23 per cent of their evening intelligence news to Communist espionage worldwide.

In 1977 (table 6), personnel and administrative problems of the CIA shared top billing with CIA covert operations abroad: together the two topics made up 57.2 per cent of the total intelligence news. Chile had sunk to twelfth place with less than 1 per cent. Again, worldwide foreign espionage (over 90 per cent Soviet-bloc) received only 5.27 per cent of the coverage. The total time devoted to intelligence continued to decline, dropping to an average of about 2 per cent for each network.

The first ten months of 1978 (table 7) follow the general pattern and time allocated to intelligence of the two preceding years, with one striking exception: foreign espionage in the United States became the lead story. Together with foreign

TABLE 5

U.S. and Foreign Intelligence TV News: 1976
(ABC, CBS, and NBC Evening News Combined)

During 1976 there were 833 TV evening news programs averaging 22.62 minutes of news each. The three networks carried 273 news items on U.S. and foreign intelligence. They are tabulated below by subject, with the total number of minutes given to each and its percentage of the total intelligence news.

Subject	Minutes	Percentage of Total
1. Personnel and Administration	66.33	14.32
2. Reforms and Reorganization	65.00	14.03
3. Information Leaks	50.17	10.83
4. U.S. Covert Operations Abroad	47.83	10.33
5. Angola	46.17	9.97
6. Investigations	37.17	7.84
7. Foreign Assassinations	36.32	8.06
8. Domestic Assassinations	29.83	6.44
9. Candidate Briefings	26.00	5.61
10. Domestic Spying	24.67	5.33
*11. Foreign Espionage in U.S.	13.17	2.84
12. Reports on Foreign Situations	8.83	1.91
13. Use of Journalists	6.17	1.33
14. Submarine Recovery	1.83	.39
*15. Foreign Espionage Outside U.S.	1.83	.39
16. Drug Tests	1.00	.22
17. Watergate	.83	.18
Total	**463.17**	

*Indicates subject related to foreign intelligence agencies, totaling 15.00 minutes or 3.23%. All other subjects are related to the CIA.

TABLE 6

U.S. AND FOREIGN INTELLIGENCE TV NEWS: 1977
(ABC, CBS, and NBC Evening News Combined)

During 1977 there were 824 TV evening news programs averaging 22.63 minutes of news each. The three networks carried 188 news items on U.S. and foreign intelligence. They are tabulated below by subject, with the total number of minutes given to each and its percentage of the total intelligence news.

Subject	Minutes	Percentage of Total
1. Personnel and Administration	114.83	29.02
2. U.S. Covert Operations Abroad	111.50	28.18
3. Drug Tests	35.00	8.85
4. Energy Estimates	32.17	8.14
5. Foreign Assassinations	19.83	5.01
*6. Foreign Espionage in U.S.	19.67	4.97
7. Domestic Spying	14.33	3.62
8. Reports on Foreign Situations	13.83	3.49
9. Watergate	10.67	2.70
10. Use of Journalists	8.33	2.10
11. Information Leaks	4.67	1.18
12. Domestic Assassinations	4.50	1.14
13. Chile	2.50	.63
14. Investigations	2.17	.55
*15. Foreign Espionage Outside U.S.	1.17	.30
16. Submarine Recovery	.50	.12
Total	**395.67**	

* Indicates subjects related to foreign intelligence agencies, totaling 20.84 minutes or 5.27%. All other subjects are related to the CIA.

TABLE 7

U.S. AND FOREIGN INTELLIGENCE TV NEWS: 1978
(ABC, CBS, and NBC Evening News Combined)

During the first ten months of 1978 (January through October), there were 705 TV evening news programs, averaging 22.61 minutes of news each. The three networks carried 173 news items on U.S. and foreign intelligence. They are tabulated below by subject, with the total number of minutes given to each and its percentage of the total intelligence news.

Subject	Minutes	Percentage of Total
*1. Foreign Espionage in U.S.	94.67	24.99
2. U.S. Covert Operations Abroad	92.33	24.37
3. Reports on Foreign Situations	58.83	15.53
*4. Foreign Espionage Outside U.S.	31.33	8.27
5. Personnel and Administration	23.67	6.25
6. Foreign Assassinations	18.50	4.88
7. Angola	11.33	2.99
8. Information Leaks	10.83	2.86
9. Investigations	7.50	1.98
10. Reforms and Reorganization	6.83	1.80
11. Watergate	6.00	1.59
12. Domestic Assassinations	6.00	1.59
13. Chile	4.67	1.23
14. Energy Estimates	4.17	1.10
15. Use of Journalists	1.67	.44
16. Submarine Recovery	.50	.13
Total	**378.83**	

* Indicates subjects related to foreign intelligence agencies, totaling 126.0 minutes or 33.26%. All other subjects are related to the CIA.

spying abroad, it constituted 33.26 per cent of the network intelligence news. This significant shift in attention was due primarily to the trials of Soviet-bloc agents in this country, along with their alleged American accomplices. (Congress, however, continued to focus primarily on curtailing the security surveillance by the CIA and the FBI of U.S. citizens in this country.) Foreign covert activities of the CIA remained the second largest story, as in 1977.

Favorable and Unfavorable Stories

In the 1974–78 period as a whole, 90.07 per cent of the intelligence news on the three networks was devoted to the CIA, while only 9.93 per cent dealt with the KGB and other Communist espionage agencies. Astonishingly, the KGB appears to have been mentioned fewer than five times during these fifty-eight months on the combined evening news programs of ABC, CBS, and NBC. In the first four years, 1974–77, 95.22 per cent of the intelligence news was devoted to the CIA and only 4.78 to the Communist agencies.

Of greater significance was the tone of news about U.S. foreign intelligence. (See table 8.) Of the 1,079 stories on U.S. agencies, overwhelmingly on the CIA but with occasional references to the Defense Intelligence Agency or the National Security Agency, only 141 stories cast their activities in a favorable light. Intelligence activities were presented in an unfavorable light in 714 stories and were reported neutrally in 224. This does not mean that all the "favorable" and "unfavorable" stories were necessarily slanted or should have been reported in another way. Obviously, a gross violation of the law by any U.S. agency is newsworthy (though the press should not knowingly report stories that endanger national security) and will cast the agency involved in an unfavorable light. But to so portray intelligence activities 68.2 per cent of the time, as the evening news reporting did, is, at the least, highly questionable. This performance becomes even more disturbing when one recalls that even senators who have been highly critical of the CIA publicly acknowledge that the great bulk of the agency's

TABLE 8

Percentage of Favorable, Neutral, and Unfavorable Stories: 1974–1978
(Carried by the ABC, CBS, and NBC TV Networks)

This table embraces 1,079 news items dealing with U.S. foreign intelligence activities. These stories total 2,126 minutes of evening news broadcast time. Each story from January 1974 through October 1978 was given a neutral, favorable, or unfavorable rating. The percentage reflects the amount of time devoted to each.

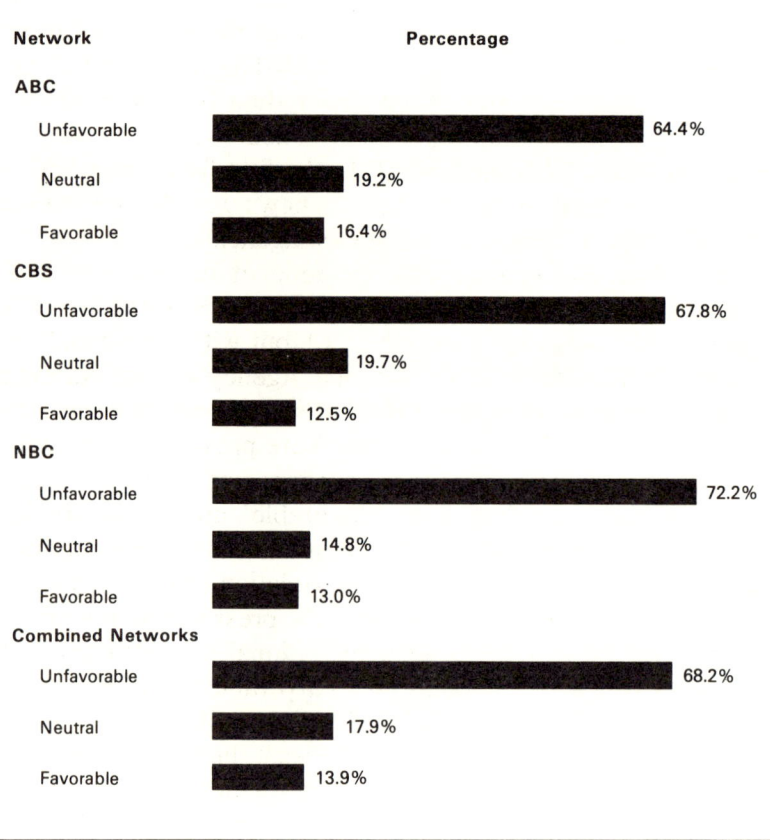

Network	Percentage
ABC	
Unfavorable	64.4%
Neutral	19.2%
Favorable	16.4%
CBS	
Unfavorable	67.8%
Neutral	19.7%
Favorable	12.5%
NBC	
Unfavorable	72.2%
Neutral	14.8%
Favorable	13.0%
Combined Networks	
Unfavorable	68.2%
Neutral	17.9%
Favorable	13.9%

activities have been conducted within its charter (the original charter appears as Appendix A) and carried out in a creditable and professional way. .

While we found no dramatic differences in either the volume or the quality of TV intelligence reporting among the networks, we did find differences in whether a particular topic was treated favorably or unfavorably. This treatment tended to change over time. Table 9 shows the volume of favorable, neutral, and unfavorable stories by time and network for 1974, 1976, and the first ten months of 1978. The table clearly indicates that all networks began with a low volume in 1974 (156.33 minutes for all networks combined) that rose sharply to 448.17 minutes in 1976 and fell back to 337.11 minutes in 1978 (assuming that the volume for the first ten months continued throughout the year).

On the favorable-unfavorable spectrum, the coverage provided by all three networks tended to moderate with time. In 1974, ABC's coverage was less in volume than the coverage by the other two and projected a more unfavorable image of U.S. intelligence. There was a steady increase in ABC's favorable stories in the 1974-78 period. By 1978, the coverage had moved from 98.3 per cent unfavorable to only 42 per cent unfavorable, compared to 63.1 unfavorable for CBS and 60.1 unfavorable for NBC the same year. During the entire period the favorable-unfavorable ratios of CBS and NBC were almost identical. The moderation evident in 1978 may suggest a greater sense of responsibility in the network news departments or merely reflect a changing public mood in the country.

Persistent Themes

Each news item on U.S. and foreign intelligence, as noted earlier, carries both information and a theme. Since the theme is a recurring idea, often a judgment or evaluation, on a current topic, it usually has a greater impact on the viewer than the reported facts. By careful analysis we found nine persistent themes in the CIA stories, five critical of the agency and four supportive. We examined a total of 1,079 CIA news items on all three evening news programs for the 1974-78 period. In these,

TABLE 9

Changes in Time Devoted to Favorable, Neutral, and Unfavorable Stories: 1974, 1976, 1978
(Carried by the ABC, CBS, and NBC TV Networks)

This table covers the same data carried in table 8, but it shows the changes in tone of stories about U.S. foreign intelligence by minutes and percentage per network for three selected years covering the span of the study.

Network	1974		1976		1978	
	Minutes	Percentage	Minutes	Percentage	Minutes	Percentage
ABC						
Favorable	0	0	25.67	17.4	27.00	23.8
Neutral	.5	1.7	34.83	23.7	38.67	34.2
Unfavorable	28.5	98.3	86.67	58.9	47.50	42.0
ABC total	29.0		147.17		113.17	
CBS						
Favorable	2.00	3.3	26.17	15.5	14.17	18.9
Neutral	6.50	10.5	46.17	27.3	13.50	18.0
Unfavorable	53.17	86.2	96.67	57.2	47.33	63.1
CBS total	61.67		169.01		75.00	
NBC						
Favorable	5.33	8.1	16.50	12.5	16.50	25.5
Neutral	5.00	7.6	33.83	25.6	9.33	14.4
Unfavorable	55.33	84.3	81.67	61.9	38.83	60.1
NBC total	65.66		132.00		64.66	
Total	156.33		448.18		252.83	

there were 831 themes critical of the CIA and 237 supportive of it. (See table 10.) The number of themes differs slightly from the number of stories because some stories had no theme while others had more than one.

By far the most persistent theme was that the CIA engages in immoral or illegal activities; this was found in 538 stories, or 50.37 per cent of the total of 1,079 stories. These news items usually dealt with domestic surveillance and other alleged violations of the rights of U.S. citizens, assassination attempts on foreign leaders and other covert activities abroad, and improper involvement in U.S. domestic politics. The theme that

TABLE 10

Major Themes in TV News Stories on U.S. Foreign Intelligence
(How the CIA was portrayed, 1974–1978)

Theme	Theme Frequency	
	Stories	Percentage
Critical of the CIA		
Engages in immoral or illegal activities	538	50.37
Is not sufficiently accountable	134	12.55
Engages in questionable activities	61	5.71
Is corrupt or untrustworthy	50	4.68
Is incompetent or ineffective	48	4.49
Subtotal	831	77.80
Supportive of the CIA		
Is endangered by excessive publicity, criticism, and political influence	76	7.13
Performs essential intelligence functions	69	6.46
Is effective and accountable	50	4.68
Seeks to maintain necessary secrecy	42	3.93
Subtotal	237	22.20
Total	1,068	100.00

Critical Themes — 77.8%
Supportive Themes — 22.2%

the CIA was not sufficiently accountable was carried by stories suggesting that the agency was uncooperative or obstructionist in dealing with Congress or the executive branch. Stories about the CIA's use of journalists, diplomats, missionaries, and dissidents to gain information supported the questionable-activities theme. The other six themes are largely self-explanatory and involve a wide range of stories.

A Lack of Perspective: The Chile Case

It is apparent from the facts presented above that most reporting about the CIA on the three evening TV news shows lacked balance, depth, and perspective. The reports gave inordinate attention to real or alleged misdeeds of the CIA to the almost total exclusion of its positive contribution to U.S.

foreign policy. There are reasons for this onesided picture other than bias, hostility, or sheer laziness in TV news departments. The CIA does not go out of its way to announce its successes because their disclosure may jeopardize the lives of the officers and agents involved or harm relations with particular governments. Yet, though good news may have been more difficult to find than bad, this does not justify the steady drumbeat of negative TV reporting.

The negative character of TV intelligence news resulted, in part, from the failure to report the *reasons* for the CIA activity abroad, whether intelligence-gathering, counterintelligence, or covert action. Further, the news stories rarely told the viewer about the circumstances that gave rise to the CIA activity being reported and interpreted by the newsmaker—be he a congressman, a journalist, or a former or present CIA officer leaking secret information.

The TV reporting of CIA activity in Chile illustrates dramatically how badly the news can be distorted when it is presented without perspective, bereft of its political and economic context. President Salvador Allende brought his Marxist Popular Unity coalition to power in 1970 with only 36.5 per cent of the popular vote. Three years later, in September 1973, he was overthrown by the Chilean armed forces that formed the regime now governing the country.

Network TV reporting on the CIA in Chile can best be seen in a cluster of twenty evening news stories in September and October 1974 that focused on both the pre-Allende and Allende periods. These stories were occasioned by the unauthorized disclosure of secret testimony on Chile in September 1974, which precipitated a congressional uproar over CIA intervention in Chile.

The following picture of CIA activity inside one of America's traditional allies emerges from these two months of ABC, CBS, and NBC evening news: For at least ten years the CIA was active in Chile, secretly trying to prevent a Marxist government from taking over. It spent $8 million between 1970 and 1973 to "destabilize" the Allende regime and helped prepare the way for the military overthrow of Allende in 1973, although it may not have participated directly in that coup. Various U.S. senators called this CIA activity unprincipled, immoral, or illegal and accused Secretary of State Henry Kissinger, CIA directors Colby and Helms, and by inference President Ford of being less than honest in their public utterances on the subject.

During this period the networks gave U.S. officials some opportunity to respond to the concerted congressional attack, but the accusers were given substantially more time to make their case. Ford, Kissinger, Colby, and Helms all "admitted" that the CIA undertook activities to keep opposition parties and the opposition press in business but said everything was done to serve U.S. national interests.

The most coherent picture, though little different in substance from earlier piecemeal reporting, was a sixteen-minute special evening report spread over October 23, 24, and 25, 1974, by NBC's John Chancellor. Neither this report nor the stories preceding it made it clear that the Allende regime was pursuing Marxist domestic and foreign policies with the close collaboration and support of Moscow and Havana. In all twenty stories, we found only one reference to the Soviet Union: on October 25, Sen. Frank Church (D.-Idaho) was reported as saying that the United States was lowering itself to the Russian level by intervening in the affairs of other states.

Wholly missing from these two months of reporting was any substantial explanation of *why* the CIA had engaged in covert activities in Chile. During the very period of the criticized CIA activity and well before, the Soviet Union and Cuba were using their military, intelligence, and trade assets to create conditions that would transform Chile into a Communist state, Cuban-style. By September 1974 these activities were a matter of public record in both Chile and the United States.[7] Soviet and Cuban subversive operations were stepped up shortly before Allende came to power and greatly accelerated immediately thereafter. It was common knowledge in Santiago that the swollen Cuban embassy was used as a coordinating center for external ideological and material support to the "revolution." The Cubans and Russians smuggled in large numbers of weapons by air and sea to arm illegal militia seeking to infiltrate and subvert the regular armed forces and to intimidate the legislature, the universities, the press, and other democratic institutions.

It was these activities by Moscow and Havana before and after Allende came to power that caused the concern of Washington officials who concluded that stability in South America and other U.S. interests were endangered by externally supported Marxist forces in Chile. In response the President authorized and ultimately ordered the CIA to act. But the millions of Americans who depend on the evening TV news were not given these simple facts. Hence they were deprived of a meaningful context and perspective for understanding what was being reported about CIA activities in Chile. Many viewers must have concluded that the CIA was shadowboxing, fighting without either an adversary or a motive.

Responsible journalism reports both the challenge and the response, but in this case the networks reported only the U.S. response—and that only partially—without defining the challenge or naming the challenger. Washington and the CIA in particular were portrayed as big bullies from North America attempting to frustrate progress or block democracy in little Chile. Without additional information no viewer would have guessed that U.S. policy, however wise or inept, was in fact intended to help democratic Chileans keep alive opposition parties, an opposition press, and an independent legislature and supreme court in the face of powerful internal and external pressures to mold Chile into a Communist totalitarian state.

Concluding Observations

1. The negative, one-sided presentation of the CIA's activities abroad—particularly covert political operations—presented in the three network evening news shows during 1974–78 both reflected and reinforced the general focus of America's "prestige press" (the *New York Times,* the *Washington Post, Time,* and *Newsweek*) for the same period.

2. Perhaps the single most striking feature of TV news on intelligence is the near absence of reporting on the espionage and covert activities of adversary states, particularly the Soviet

Union. During the 1974-78 period, we could not find as many as five references to the KGB. In the first four years of this period, slightly less than 5 per cent of the intelligence news on network TV was devoted to Soviet-bloc agencies, while slightly more than 95 per cent was focused on the CIA. The result was a distorted view of reality. The CIA appeared to be operating in a political and moral vacuum devoid of threats and adversaries. It was a villainous Don Quixote tilting at vaporous windmills.

In 1978 the picture changed somewhat. The networks gave 33.26 per cent of their intelligence time to adversary activities, largely in their coverage of U.S. trials of Soviet-bloc agents. This upsurge of attention to Communist espionage was probably a temporary aberration rather than evidence of a decision to provide adequate information on the hostile environment in which U.S. intelligence is forced to operate.

3. The one-sided portrait of the CIA emerged from the tendency to stress the negative and downplay the positive. In 1,079 stories on the CIA carried by the networks during 1974-78, only 13.9 per cent (measured in minutes) reflected favorably on the CIA; 17.9 per cent were neutral, and 68.2 per cent reflected unfavorably. (See table 8.)

4. When the stories are analyzed by themes, the distortion becomes even more evident. The five themes critical of the CIA constituted 77.8 per cent of the total, the supportive themes, 22.2 per cent. Almost 69 per cent of the stories reported that the CIA engaged in immoral, illegal, or questionable activities or was not sufficiently accountable, while only slightly over 11 per cent reported that the CIA performed essential intelligence functions or was accountable.

5. The networks did not differ significantly in the volume of intelligence reporting they carried on their evening news shows over the 1974-78 period, but they did differ in the percentage of favorable vs. unfavorable stories about the CIA. In 1974, 98.3 per cent of ABC's stories (measured in minutes) were unfavorable, but by 1978 this dropped to 42.0. Both CBS and NBC had about 85 per cent unfavorable stories in 1974; by the end of the period they too had lowered this percentage, but less dramatically. (See table 9.)

6. The ABC, CBS, and NBC evening news shows failed to provide their millions of viewers with the facts, background, and perspective they needed to understand the role of intelligence in U.S. foreign policy. The citizen-viewer, for example, was denied an adequate picture of the dangers facing the United States and its allies from the Soviet Union and its collaborators. The viewer was never adequately informed about the vital importance of U.S. intelligence—collection, counterintelligence, and covert activity—or about situations of special danger to our national interests. In sum, the TV networks did not observe the spirit of the Fairness Doctrine or the letter of their own *Code of Broadcast News Ethics,* which says that news should be "accurate and comprehensive" and presented with sufficient information to provide "meaning and perspective."[8] They fell far short of what a free and democratic society has a right to expect of its communications media.

Afterword

CHARLES M. LICHENSTEIN

THE FOUR CHAPTERS OF this book speak for themselves. I will simply sum up each of them briefly and then, using their arguments as a foundation, speculate along a few additional lines and identify three principal future options for the U.S. intelligence community.

Chapter 1 affirms that a strong, effective, thoroughly professional intelligence capability is an indispensable instrument of U.S. national purpose and policy in the world, particularly in the face of grave threats to the nation's security and that of its allies. Such a "full service" intelligence capability necessarily includes the collection of information by clandestine means, both human and technical; counterintelligence; covert operations; and, at the apex, the production of finished intelligence which provides estimates of the resources and intentions of other nations. Moreover, by extrapolation from the "just war" theory, a U.S. intelligence establishment which combines all of these mutually supporting components is defensible and indeed *required* on moral as well as pragmatic grounds.

The role of the U.S. Congress is the focus of chapter 2. Beginning about five years ago—to a significant extent as fallout from the national traumas of Vietnam and Watergate, and a pervasive iconoclasm regarding all of the established institutions of American society—Congress has been attempting to put tight reins on the allegedly inadequately controlled intelligence agencies, especially the CIA, and particularly in the areas of clandestine collection and covert operations. This unprecedented congressional involvement in both the processes and substance of the "closed world" of foreign intelligence has taken the form of widely publicized investigations, sensational disclosures, restrictive legislation, rigorous oversight, and some additional statutory protection of the civil rights of Americans—and the end is not yet in sight.

The congressional effort, as noted in chapter 3, has been abetted, even spearheaded, by an interlocking network of individuals and organizations—which constitutes a quite literal "anti-intelligence lobby"—whose openly stated intention is to diminish if not abolish existing U.S. capabilities in clandestine collection, counterintelligence, and particularly covert operations. This aggressive, well-organized, well-financed lobby, a curious amalgam of "respectables" and extremists, has had an inordinate influence in defining the agenda of reform. It has been rather weakly opposed by a relative handful of former intelligence professionals with very modest resources, and by a few members of the academic community acting as individuals.

The role of television is analyzed in chapter 4. Insofar as the U.S. public has been informed about these matters by the evening television network news programs—which some two-thirds of the public identifies as its principal and most trusted news source—it has received information which is sketchy, superficial, out of meaningful context (or rather, in no particular context at all), and tilted generally toward anti-intelligence themes. Intelligence as "rogue elephant" has received lurid treatment; intelligence as the quiet collector of information and interpreter of events, more academic than derring-do in character, has received scarcely any. Typical of television news in general, the coverage has been largely a headline service which has waxed and waned with the primacy—and the sensationalism—of "the intelligence story." There has been little consistency in it and less depth.

Further Observations

Moving now somewhat beyond the compass of these four chapters, each of which is amply documented and stands on its own, it is possible to speculate along a few additional lines.

Diminished capabilities. No one on the outside can ever be certain about this, but it does seem clear that the net effect of five years' calculated assault on U.S. intelligence agencies has been to diminish their capabilities severely—in the clandestine services especially. Sources have been compromised, and many have dried up altogether. Credibility has been damaged. Productive careers have been aborted, or not entered into at all. Long lead-time infrastructure—so critically important to covert operations—has been permitted to deteriorate, or has not been built. Lives have been put in jeopardy.

Nor can the clandestine services be isolated from the finished product of intelligence analysis. The two move together; they inform, guide, and enrich each other. As the capabilities of the former have been diminished, it seems only reasonable to conclude that the quality, authority, and reliability of the latter have suffered as well.

At the same time it would be wrong to try to conclude too much. Are the "losses" of Iran and Nicaragua, for example, and the "sudden discovery" of Soviet combat troops in Cuba, fairly characterized as "intelligence failures"? Or is this scapegoating? Should these incidents instead be laid to failures of *will* on the part of our national leaders, to failures of *policy?* We cannot be sure. Sound and timely intelligence may be prerequisite to wise and effective national security policy—but it can never guarantee that the resulting policy will be wise *or* effective.

These are impressions only. Yet there is substantial evidence that they are valid. Even if intelligence professionals and former directors of Central Intelligence are dismissed as tendentious and unreliable witnesses, the letter of the law (see chapter 2) and the flavor of congressional reports (the latest of which, although highly classified, was leaked in mid-1979) strongly indicate that the U.S. foreign intelligence services are now operating under severe handicaps—and that the assault of the last five years has not yet run its course.

The great non-debate. Just to sharpen the points at issue, let's assume that the U.S. intelligence community in some part deserves this assault—that the public has lost patience with what it perceives as the intelligence agencies' sophomoric ineptitude, their incessant bureaucratic fratricide, and sometimes their serious invasions of the constitutionally protected rights of Americans. Even if this were so, questions would have to be raised.

One, obviously, is whether and to what extent such a public perception would have any foundation—whether most or some or even a barely significant number of the allegations of improprieties are accurate. This question goes to the selectivity of the "facts" which congressional critics have chosen to spread on the public record and, of these, which ones the news media have chosen to highlight. Put the other way around: what does the public *not* know about intelligence—what does it not know about the painstaking research and analysis and about the conspicuous "success stories" of the clandestine services? Were it available to the public, how would this kind of information weigh in the balance of public judgment?

An even more basic question has to be raised—namely, when is the great public debate *about intelligence* going to begin? Not about the limits of executive power, or "no more Vietnams," or even "no more Chiles" (where the public record suggests that the CIA was on the whole carrying out orders, whatever the merits of those orders might have been). If there is a principal conclusion that emerges sharply from the record of these last five years, it is that there has been almost no genuine debate about intelligence at all. There has been some lip-service to the "need" for intelligence, but the threshold questions have scarcely been addressed, much less examined in depth:

• What *is* intelligence? What functions does it typically perform?

• Who needs it and for what? What kinds of capabilities does it provide to policy-makers, and what happens (or does not happen) in their absence?

• How much of it and what kinds are needed, and at what expenditure of both dollars and risks?

• How does the total process operate? How should the vari-

ous intelligence functions relate to one another? How should they be managed, and how controlled?
- What are the preconditions and prerequisites of an effective intelligence service, and what exceptions have to be made to the normal democratic process—what conscious departures, if any, from the democratic model of conducting the public's business in full sunshine and strict accord with the norms of gentlemanly behavior?

These are the kinds of questions that would be addressed in a debate worthy of the name. For the most part, they simply have not been.

Even more, there has been over these last five years no real debate about intelligence as an instrument of national purpose and policy *in this world*—assuming, to be sure, that the United States has purposes which it seeks to achieve by means of rational policies, that these purposes are legitimized by values which the vast majority of Americans believes to be grounded in truth and justice, and that there are powerful forces around the world determined to thwart these purposes and undermine these values.

There are those, of course, who tend to dismiss this set of assumptions as the outmoded worldview of unreconstructed cold warriors. And there may be some truth in this—although just how "outmoded" the perception of a continuing Communist threat might be is at the very least an open question. There is a strong correlation—both conceptually and existentially—between those who believe that the assault on U.S. intelligence agencies has exceeded all reasonable bounds and those who believe (1) that the United States is seeking to protect its national interests and promote its national values in an external environment filled with peril, and (2) that it is not only prudent but also an affirmative moral obligation of this nation to promote its values—that the world is both a safer and more humane place when people are free of oppression and free to govern themselves than when these freedoms are denied. Insofar as a strong intelligence capability is an important instrument in the pursuit of such goals, the correlation is doubtless more than coincidental.

Yet it is hard to conceive of any U.S. government, whatever its ideological orientation, which would have no need—and feel none—for a reliable source of information about the world we inhabit (information drawn from more than just open sources) and, in all likelihood, for an effective covert instrument as an adjunct to its diplomacy and military power. It is not so much a particular ideological orientation that leads to the need for a solid intelligence capability as it is sheer ignorance of the outside world and the natural desire of any group of policy-makers to operate on the basis of reliable estimates of the resources and intentions of other governments, friendly and hostile. If intelligence agencies did not exist, they would indeed have to be invented.

Options for the Future

Where do we go from here? What might happen next? There would seem to be three principal options for the future:

1. One possibility is that "this too shall pass" and that the U.S. intelligence community will go back to doing business as usual, pre-1974—except that this simply is *not* possible. It has to be ruled out on political grounds alone. There is almost no chance that the restrictive legislation now on the books will be erased in the foreseeable future, and even less that Congress will want to surrender its deep involvement in the intelligence process. (There may be some possibility that, in due time, Congress will decide to impose limits on itself—on the extent and depth of its involvement. This is an intriguing and open question.)

Then, too, the past cannot simply be waived away: substantial damage has been done to U.S. intelligence; older, pre-1974 capabilities have deteriorated, and new ones have not been developed; professional morale has been shaken, if not shattered; time has been lost, and that, in a very real sense, can never be recovered. The effects of the last five years will remain with us for a long time to come.

2. It seems almost as unlikely—possible but not very—that the present uneasy equilibrium will hold. This is the second

possible option for the future: that in whatever weakened state, U.S. intelligence will go on and operate as best it can. This seems improbable for two quite contrary reasons. From the one side, there is little apparent let-up in the effort to pass increasingly more restrictive legislation, to rein in the intelligence agencies even more tightly, and to diminish (or abolish) covert action capabilities in particular. Certainly these efforts will continue.

From the other side, there is some evidence (including hints in the nation's prestige press, in *Time,* for example, and the *Washington Post* and the *Wall Street Journal*) of a backlash developing: our intelligence capabilities *are* diminished, and that is beginning to be perceived as unacceptable. Important members of Congress share this view. Either way, it appears that the battle has not yet run its course and that there are some critical issues still to be fought out.

3. This apparent disequilibrium does open up a third option: it is just possible that a genuine debate about intelligence may now begin. From the perspective of intelligence *per se,* there are questions worth debating and reforms worth considering. These are not new questions. They have been just below the surface of the controversy all along. It may be, for example, that the clandestine services are too much in control of the agencies' priorities, and that they tend to influence "self-fulfilling" analyses. It may be that the entire intelligence community is badly organized—even that the clandestine services should be separated from the research-and-analysis branches. Certainly there would seem to be a need for some manner and degree of congressional oversight of the intelligence process—reasonable, responsible, focused on the broad policy which should both direct and control the agencies.

These are just a few examples. The answers are not obvious. But there does appear to be a genuine agenda of reform, not necessarily the one set by the anti-intelligence lobby, that deserves serious debate. It is never too late to begin.

In another sense, the real debate will in fact *not* be about intelligence at all. It will be about how the American people and their leaders perceive this nation's role in the world. In this sense, the correlation referred to before is far from coincidental: it is of the essence. Insofar as the United States is serious about its responsibilities as a great power—to its allies, to itself, to its best sense of what it takes for the world to become reasonably "safe for freedom"—the debate about intelligence will be deeply affected. Answers to the prior question will not determine every minute detail of how our intelligence services should be organized and controlled. But they will speak to the primacy of intelligence as an instrument of serious national purpose.

The first chapter stated that the purpose of this book was to study the adequacy or inadequacy of the *debate* over intelligence in a free society. "Is this debate grounded in a clear sense of our national purposes and a realistic appreciation of the resources and instruments necessary to fulfill them?" The answers, so far, would seem to be "no"—the debate has been neither adequate nor grounded in a clear sense of national purpose. But, to repeat, it is never too late to begin.

APPENDIX A

The National Security Act of 1947

In 1947 Congress enacted a National Security Act "to provide a comprehensive program for the future security of the United States." The act created the Department of Defense, the National Security Council, and the Central Intelligence Agency. Excerpts from the act as amended are reproduced below from "Organizing for National Security," an inquiry of the Subcommittee on National Policy Machinery for the Senate Committee on Government Operations, 1961, volume 2, pages 119-23. (Footnotes have been omitted.)

DECLARATION OF POLICY

SEC. 2. In enacting this legislation, it is the intent of Congress to provide a comprehensive program for the future security of the United States; to provide for the establishment of integrated policies and procedures for the departments, agencies, and functions of the Government relating to the national security; to provide a Department of Defense, including the three military Departments of the Army, the Navy (including naval aviation and the United States Marine Corps), and the Air Force under the direction, authority, and control of the Secretary of Defense; to provide that each military department shall be separately organized under its own Secretary and shall function under the direction, authority, and control of the Secretary of Defense; to provide for their unified direction under civilian control of the Secretary of Defense but not to merge these departments or services; to provide for the establishment of unified or specified combatant commands, and a clear and direct line of command to such commands; to eliminate unnecessary duplication in the Department of Defense, and particularly in the field of research and engineering by vesting its overall direction and control in the Secretary of Defense; to provide more effective, efficient, and economical administration in the Department of Defense; to provide for the unified strategic direction of the combatant forces, for their operation under unified command, and for their integration into an efficient team of land, naval, and air forces but not to establish a single Chief of Staff over the armed forces nor an overall armed forces general staff.

128   NATIONAL SECURITY ACT

TITLE I—COORDINATION FOR NATIONAL SECURITY

NATIONAL SECURITY COUNCIL

SEC. 101. (a) There is hereby established a council to be known as the National Security Council (hereinafter in this section referred to as the "Council").

The President of the United States shall preside over meetings of the Council: *Provided,* That in his absence he may designate a member of the Council to preside in his place.

The function of the Council shall be to advise the President with respect to the integration of domestic, foreign, and military policies relating to the national security so as to enable the military services and the other departments and agencies of the Government to cooperate more effectively in matters involving the national security.

The Council shall be composed of—
 (1) the President;
 (2) the Vice President;
 (3) the Secretary of State;
 (4) the Secretary of Defense;
 (5) [position subsequently abolished]
 (6) the Director of the Office of Civil and Defense Mobilization;
 (7) the Secretaries and Under Secretaries of other executive departments and of the military departments, when appointed by the President by and with the advice and consent of the Senate, to serve at his pleasure.

(b) In addition to performing such other functions as the President may direct, for the purpose of more effectively coordinating the policies and functions of the departments and agencies of the Government relating to the national security, it shall, subject to the direction of the President, be the duty of the Council—
 (1) to assess and appraise the objectives, commitments, and risks of the United States in relation to our actual and potential military power, in the interest of national security, for the purpose of making recommendations to the President in connection therewith; and
 (2) to consider policies on matters of common interest to the departments and agencies of the Government concerned with the national security, and to make recommendations to the President in connection therewith.

(c) The Council shall have a staff to be headed by a civilian executive secretary who shall be appointed by the President, and who shall receive compensation at the rate of [$10,000] [$15,000] $20,000 a year. The executive secretary, subject to the direction of the Council, is hereby authorized, subject to the civil-service laws and the Classification Act of 1923, as amended, to appoint and fix the compensation of such personnel as may be necessary to perform such duties as may be prescribed by the Council in connection with the performance of its functions.

(d) The Council shall, from time to time, make such recommendations, and such other reports to the President as it deems appropriate or as the President may require.

CENTRAL INTELLIGENCE AGENCY

SEC. 102. (a) There is hereby established under the National Security Council a Central Intelligence Agency with a Director of Central Intelligence who shall be the head thereof, and with a Deputy Director of Central Intelligence who shall act for, and exercise the powers of, the Director during his absence or disability. The Director and the Deputy Director shall be appointed by the President, by and with the advice and consent of the Senate, from among the commissioned officers of the armed services, whether in an active or retired status, or from among individuals in civilian life: *Provided, however,* That at no time shall the two positions of the Director and Deputy Director be occupied simultaneously by commissioned officers of the armed services, whether in an active or retired status.

(b) (1) If a commissioned officer of the armed services is appointed as Director, or Deputy Director, then—

(A) in the performance of his duties as Director, or Deputy Director, he shall be subject to no supervision, control, restriction, or prohibition (military or otherwise) other than would be operative with respect to him if he were a civilian in no way connected with the Department of the Army, the Department of the Navy, the Department of the Air Force, or the armed services or any component thereof; and

(B) he shall not possess or exercise any supervision, control, powers, or functions (other than such as he possesses, or is authorized or directed to exercise, as Director, or Deputy Director) with respect to the armed services or any component thereof, the Department of the Army, the Department of the Navy, or the Department of the Air Force, or any branch, bureau, unit, or division thereof, or with respect to any of the personnel (military or civilian) of any of the foregoing.

(2) Except as provided in paragraph (1), the appointment to the office of Director, or Deputy Director, of a commissioned officer of the armed services, and his acceptance of and service in such office, shall in no way affect any status, office, rank, or grade he may occupy or hold in the armed services, or any emolument, perquisite, right, privilege, or benefit incident to or arising out of any such status, office, rank, or grade. Any such commissioned officer shall, while serving in the office of Director, or Deputy Director, continue to hold rank and grade not lower than that in which serving at the time of his appointment and to receive the military pay and allowances (active or retired,

as the case may be, including personal money allowances) payable to a commissioned officer of his grade and length of service for which the appropriate department shall be reimbursed from any fund available to defray the expenses of the Central Intelligence Agency. He shall be paid by the Central Intelligence Agency from such funds an annual compensation at a rate equal to the amount by which the compensation established for such position exceeds the amount of his annual military pay and allowances.

(3) The rank or grade of any such commissioned officer shall, during the period in which such commissioned officer occupies the office of Director of Central Intelligence, or Deputy Director of Central Intelligence, be in addition to the numbers and percentages otherwise authorized and appropriated for the armed service of which he is a member.

(c) Notwithstanding the provisions of section 6 of the Act of August 24, 1912 (37 Stat. 555), or the provisions of any other law, the Director of Central Intelligence may, in his discretion, terminate the employment of any officer or employee of the Agency whenever he shall deem such termination necessary or advisable in the interests of the United States, but such termination shall not affect the right of such officer or employee to seek or accept employment in any other department or agency of the Government if declared eligible for such employment by the United States Civil Service Commission.

(d) For the purpose of coordinating the intelligence activities of the several Government departments and agencies in the interest of national security, it shall be the duty of the Agency, under the direction of the National Security Council—

(1) to advise the National Security Council in matters concerning such intelligence activities of the Government departments and agencies as relate to national security;

(2) to make recommendations to the National Security Council for the coordination of such intelligence activities of the departments and agencies of the Government as relate to the national security;

(3) to correlate and evaluate intelligence relating to the national security, and provide for the appropriate dissemination of such intelligence within the Government using where appropriate, existing agencies and facilities: *Provided,* That the Agency shall have no police, subpena, law-enforcement powers, or internal-security functions: *Provided further,* That the departments and other agencies of the Government shall continue to collect, evaluate, correlate, and disseminate departmental intelligence: *And provided further,* That the Director of Central Intelligence shall be responsible for protecting intelligence sources and methods from unauthorized disclosure;

(4) to perform, for the benefit of the existing intelligence agencies, such additional services of common concern as the National Security Council determines can be more efficiently accomplished centrally;

(5) to perform such other functions and duties related to intelligence affecting the national security as the National Security Council may from time to time direct.

(e) To the extent recommended by the National Security Council and approved by the President, such intelligence of the departments and agencies of the Government, except as hereinafter provided, relating to the national security shall be open to the inspection of the Director of Central Intelligence, and such intelligence as relates to the national security and is possessed by such departments and other agencies of the Government, except as hereinafter provided, shall be made available to the Director of Central Intelligence for correlation, evaluation, and dissemination: *Provided, however,* That upon the written request of the Director of Central Intelligence, the Director of the Federal Bureau of Investigation shall make available to the Director of Central Intelligence such information for correlation, evaluation, and dissemination as may be essential to the national security.

(f) Effective when the Director first appointed under subsection (a) has taken office—

(1) the National Intelligence Authority (11 Fed. Reg. 1337, 1339, February 5, 1946) shall cease to exist; and

(2) The personnel, property, and records of the Central Intelligence Group are transferred to the Central Intelligence Agency, and such group shall cease to exist. Any unexpended balances of appropriations, allocations, or other funds available or authorized to be made available for such Group shall be available and shall be authorized to be made available in like manner for expenditure by the Agency.

APPENDIX B

KGB Activities in the United States

HOWARD HANDLEMAN

This journalistic account of recent Soviet KGB activities in America provides useful background information for the reader of this volume; it is not presented as a complete or scholarly treatment of the subject. The author, a veteran Washington and foreign correspondent, was on the staff of "U.S. News and World Report" from 1960 to 1978. The article appeared under the title "The Soviet KGB in America" in the June 1979 issue of "Air Force Magazine," published by the Air Force Association in Washington, D.C., and is reprinted by permission.

AT THE VERY TIME that American counterintelligence is under attack at home, the Soviet Union's spy service, the KGB, is mounting a major offensive on this country.

Since 1966, the Soviet government has doubled the number of its espionage agents in the United States. In the past year, the Kremlin has stepped up the pace. And Washington is the battlefield for this cloak-and-dagger war.

Meanwhile, U.S. counterintelligence forces are on the decline. A knowledgeable assessment of the problem comes from W. Raymond Wannall, former Assistant Director for Intelligence for the Federal Bureau of Investigation: "Fifteen or twenty years ago, we used to average about four FBI counterintelligence agents for every known or suspected Soviet agent. Now, the ratio is down to one to one, or even a bit less."

That gives reason to doubt that the United States can keep up with KGB agents in America. A counterintelligence authority says it takes ten to fifteen men to shadow a single enemy agent. Sometimes, far more are needed. About 140 FBI agents were in on the arrest of US Navy Yeoman Nelson Drummond in 1962. Drummond was convicted of espionage charges and sentenced to life imprisonment. About the same number were used the following year when the FBI caught the American engineer, John Butenko, who was convicted and sentenced to thirty years.

Intelligence Targets

Targets of the KGB—the Committee for State Security—have been altered over the years. A dozen years ago, the KGB focused on getting information about the intentions of the United States and its allies, with the basic question being: "What are they going to do next?"

The KGB still keeps this target in mind, but there has been a shifting of priorities. Today, the emphasis is on policies with international connotation, with less concern for domestic programs with no direct impact beyond U.S. borders. FBI Director William M. Webster was speaking of the KGB in a recent speech in Chicago when he said:

"The interests of foreign governments center primarily upon technological, political, and scientific intelligence, as well as economic, sociological, and geographic information. Also of interest is personal information about individuals who have the capability of setting opinions or who might be recruited by a foreign power in an effort to gain additional information of value.

"Obtaining our most recent scientific advances in areas such as microelectronics, computers, lasers, nuclear energy, and, of course, military and space technology is the major thrust of this activity."

Counterintelligence agents say current KGB priorities place industrial secrets high on the list of targets. This international version of industrial espionage subverts U.S. efforts to control the transfer abroad of technology with military applications.

Mr. Webster's reference to "personal information" reflects the KGB search for Americans in key spots who have an exploitable weakness. KGB agents know they have a better chance of subverting an engineer who is a homosexual, a military officer with a yen for wine or women, or a diplomat who needs money.

Recruiting spies is a prime function of a KGB agent. He looks for two types: the person of influence, and the person with access to confidential documents. Government employees are the favored targets, but scientists, engineers, even hotel maids, and others also are objects of recruiting efforts.

A low-ranking person, like CIA watch officer Michael Kampiles, can be especially useful, if he has access to important documents. Kampiles is appealing a conviction for selling to the Soviets a manual detailing secrets about a U.S. satellite. In the eyes of the KGB, such documents are far superior to a spy's verbal report.

Counting Spies

The numbers of KGB agents and their allies alone are enough to cause concern. As one yardstick, the Soviet Union and its Warsaw Pact allies have twice as many official personnel in this country now as they did a dozen years ago. These are not only diplomatic personnel but also others who are posted to the United States.

The FBI's Webster says the exact number of Soviet and other Communist agents is unknown, "but you may be sure that the number is greater than the number of our own special agents assigned to foreign counterintelligence work."

There are about 1,900 Soviet-bloc officials currently on assignment in the United States. These include not only diplomats, but employees of the Soviet Union's TASS news agency and other Soviet news correspondents, of Amtorg and other trading companies, and of other Soviet and Warsaw Pact missions that keep personnel permanently posted to the United States.

The FBI estimates that forty percent of the people in the United States on Soviet or Warsaw Pact passports are professionals assigned to the KGB or other Communist spy units. That would mean about 760 full-time professional agents. But that's not all. The FBI assumes that the remaining sixty-five to seventy percent of the officials in the United States representing Warsaw Pact countries are forced to work at least part-time on Soviet intelligence chores. That's another 800 agents the United States must keep an eye on.

And there are more, including:

- **Merchant seamen.** Forty American ports have been opened to Soviet-bloc merchantmen since 1972. About 20,000 Soviet-bloc seamen annually have the freedom of the ports on shore leave. The FBI assumes there are spies among them, but nobody knows how many.
- **Delegations and other visitors.** This category includes exchange students, scientists, technicians, trade groups, educators, artists, and others who regularly make the trek to America. The FBI assumption is that KGB officials or agents of the GRU, the Red Army spy organization, are with every group. One function of these agents is to keep an eye out for defectors. Another, particularly among trade missions visiting American industrial plants, is to spy. All told, 30,000 Soviet-bloc visitors came to the United States last year. And U.S. counterspies are frank to say the number of spies among them is unknown and unknowable.

Then there are "illegals" who slip into the country with forged or stolen passports. KGB Col. Rudolf Abel was one of them. He conducted spy operations in New York for more than eight years before he was exposed.

Cuban Cooperation

Also among the "illegals" are Cuban agents, posing as refugees, but actually in the employ of Cuba's Dirección Generale de Inteligencia (DGI) for the Soviet KGB. They are made welcome in the unsuspecting communities of the 700,000 or so legitimate refugees from Fidel Castro's Cuba. These "illegals" have advantages over KGB agents from the Soviet Union. They can melt into the Cuban population and need no training to disguise their origin. Some reveal themselves only when they return to Cuba. By then, however, it is too late for U.S. counterintelligence to act. The FBI doesn't even have an estimate as to how many Cuban spy "illegals" there are in America.

Russian espionage has a long history. The Okhrana, the Czar's dread secret police, worked against dissidents and revolutionaries in nineteenth and twentieth century Russia. When the revolutionaries went abroad, so did the Okhrana, to infiltrate and spy on emigré conspiratorial groups.

The Communists carried on in the same tradition after they took over the government in 1917. Some of the Czar's spies, in fact, were recruited by the Communists for their newly formed Cheka. The Cheka quickly became as feared as the Okhrana, and for much the same reasons.

Cheka was succeeded by a whole series of organizations. But while the names changed, the duties, functions, and authority remained constant. Among them were the GPU, OGPU, NKVD, MGB, MVD, and, today, the KGB.

The KGB came into existence on March 13, 1954, as part of the governmental overhaul that followed the death of Joseph Stalin just a year before. It took over the more important duties, functions, and authority of the MVD. The MVD, Ministry of Internal Affairs, was relegated to more routine police and fire-fighting duties.

U.S. counterintelligence experts say the KGB is responsible for border guards, the internal secret police, the watch over all military and some of the more sensitive industrial units, and, of course, the espionage agents and spymasters sent abroad. The U.S. intelligence community estimates KGB's total manpower at 400,000. Close ties with Warsaw Pact countries, Cuba, and other Soviet satellites provide many more agents.

One key advantage the KGB once had but now is losing is the ability to recruit Americans—as well as others—for idealistic reasons. This phenomenon is hard to measure, but the evidence of a decline is clear to the experts. One authority explains: "The Soviets no longer inspire people as they did in the 1920s and 1930s. KGB can buy, flatter, seduce, or blackmail a spy. But communism has been so discredited in the West that Soviet agents no longer can get many to work for them for reasons of Communist ideology."

This does not mean Americans cannot be recruited, but the motivation is likely to be other than Communist ideals.

Motivation to Spy

One counterintelligence authority says bitterness over the Vietnam War, for example, can serve as a motivation. People who are disenchanted with American values because of the war may be potential spies for the Soviet Union, not out of love for the Soviet system, but in reaction against the United States, counterintelligence experts claim.

The KGB also is benefiting from current public opinion demanding "clean hands" in counterintelligence and intelligence operations, a trend attributed to reaction not only to the Vietnam War, but also to the Watergate scandal.

Today, eight groups in Congress oversee CIA and FBI operations: House and Senate committees on Appropriations, Armed Services, Foreign Affairs, and Intelligence. The committees together have more than 200 members. Some serve on more than one committee. In addition, hundreds of staff members working for the committees or for individual members have access to the kind of sensitive information that is a target of the KGB.

But federal security procedures that protect and restrict such information do not fully apply on Capitol Hill. Congressmen themselves are not investigated for security clearances. They are "cleared" automatically for the most secret information by the simple fact of their election.

Staff members are cleared if they need to handle classified information. But government security officials express concern that others do not require clearance, even though they may be working in an office where classified material is available. Some of the most secret information of the government is made available to members of Congress.

KGB officers make frequent and open visits to congressional offices. They collect the published records of hearings on foreign affairs, military weaponry, the budget, or any of the many other subjects that are of interest to the Soviets. It is all legal, but it annoys many congressmen and staffers.

Some KGB operations on the Hill are illegal, however, such as attempting to listen in on closed-door hearings. Government agencies, at the request of congressional committees, make it a practice to examine a hearing room before classified information is discussed. Such "sweeps" have turned up "bugs"—electronic listening devices.

U.S. experts say other targets of KGB agents are the stenotypists who work for commercial companies hired to make transcripts of hearings for Congress. These firms must satisfy government security standards before they are considered for contracts.

Counterintelligence experts say these and similar efforts to exploit such potential sources of intelligence have been uncovered. Secret testimony in Congress could enable the Kremlin to learn whether the United States is planning a new missile, what is being proposed in new defense programs, or what changes are being considered in strategic plans for the defense of the nation.

Soviet Audacity

Another way of gathering intelligence on the Hill is to quiz the people who work there. One Senate staffer tells of conversations with Russians: "They come all the time, but the number increases with the urgency of the information they want. You can see them asking the same groups of questions, as though they had memorized them. When U.S. relations with China were coming to a head, the Soviets literally swarmed over the Hill."

Offsetting the potential for espionage on the Hill has been the patriotism of Hill employees. Mr. Wannall says that while he headed counterintelligence for the FBI, many staffers in congressional offices and committees willingly cooperated with his agents. Counterintelligence sources say a number of Hill staffers have acted as double agents, pretending to cooperate with the KGB, while reporting to the FBI.

Other government agencies, including the State Department and the Pentagon, are also KGB targets. To penetrate these departments, the Freedom of Information Act is used, not only by American citizens, but also by foreigners. CIA Director Stansfield Turner tells of getting a request for sensitive information from the Polish Embassy, the first Soviet-bloc country to use the act. As the report requested was not classified, the agency was required by law to release it.

The Freedom of Information Act has been a source of complaints among government security officials partly because of the increased danger of inadvertently releasing sensitive information. A number of cases have occurred where release of documents, supposedly cleared of sensitive information, allowed criminal suspects and foreign agents to figure out the identity of informants.

The KGB also tries to buy information, or to bribe Americans to hand over sensitive materials. In one case, a company made an offer to help an American firm with a Navy contract that dealt with classified material. The offer, made through the mail, seemed legitimate. But a check revealed there was no such company.

Secret Documents

The KGB here and its center in Moscow put the greatest value on documents classified "secret" or "top secret." That is why a Michael Kampiles, who didn't rank high in the eyes of the CIA, ranked very high on the KGB target list.

Army SFC Jack Edward Dunlap didn't have access to such documents. But he knew a secretary who did. Dunlap was a messenger in the top-secret National Security Agency that devises communications codes for the U.S. government and tries to break the codes of other governments.

The secretary's job required her to pick up documents in another part of the sprawling NSA headquarters building. Dunlap, after gaining her confidence, suggested that he could pick up the papers and take them to her, as he had to walk by them in the normal course of his job. His government clearance as a messenger satisfied established security regulations. She accepted. What he didn't say was that he had a market for copies—the KGB. FBI officials said he was paid $60,000, over several years, for delivering copies of the highly classified documents. He blew the money on a cabin cruiser, a racing hydroplane, two Cadillacs and a Jaguar, and other luxuries. It is thought he began to feed secrets to the Soviets in 1960. He committed suicide on July 23, 1963, when the FBI was on his trail.

The KGB is so eager for classified American information that some Americans have collected Soviet money for innocuous papers on which they stamped "secret" or "top secret."

To penetrate U.S. security in Washington, KGB agents loiter in the bars of better hotels, where VIP visitors check in. Their object is to eavesdrop and to spot potential recruits. In the hotels they also attempt to recruit maids and bellboys, who have ready access with passkeys to guest rooms.

In the bars, KGB agents strike up casual conversations with Americans, and pick up a name, or some detail about their work. "Every little bit helps," says one expert. "They can fit it in with other things that are heard and reported. The American doesn't have to be in government. He can work for a contractor and still unwittingly provide valuable information."

U.S. Political Parties

Another target of KGB agents is people in political parties, particularly promising young people. The KGB sometimes will place a "sleeper" agent with a politician as a volunteer worker. If the politician wins office, the "sleeper" is in a good position to be hired.

In one case, a young lawyer was elected to the New York State Legislature. A member of the Soviet mission to the United Nations approached him and asked him to do some legal work. It wasn't much—but the Soviet agent paid about three times what it was worth. This was followed by more job offers and more extravagant payments. The payments became so extravagant that the lawyer became suspicious and reported them to the FBI.

Then there is the case of James Frederick Sattler. Born in New York, he had a promising career as a political scientist. He studied in Germany and Poland; taught in New Zealand, Canada, Germany, and France; and did business in Britain, Switzerland, and other European countries.

When he worked for the pro-NATO Atlantic Council in Washington, he was known as being too anti-Communist and was cautioned several times about this tendency. The Council later gave him an excellent recommendation when he applied for a job with the International Security Subcommittee, a sensitive section of the House International Relations Committee.

His career fell apart when Rep. Paul Findley (R-Ill.) asked the FBI to check on him. The FBI didn't have to check. It already knew that for years Sattler had been working for East Germany. Alerted by the Committee rejection, he immediately registered as an East German agent, signing and swearing to the registration statement on March 23, 1976. He told authorities he was recruited in 1967 by a man who said he represented the Warsaw Pact Association. Later he learned that the recruiter was linked to the Central Committee of the Socialist Unity Party, the East German Communist Party.

Over the years he was paid $15,000 and decorated by the East German Ministry for State Security. For more than eight years, Sattler said, he transmitted "information and documents which I received from the North Atlantic Treaty Organization and from individuals in institutions and government

KGB ACTIVITIES IN THE UNITED STATES 139

agencies in the Federal Republic of Germany, United States, Great Britain, Canada, and France."

He confessed he had been photographing information with a microdisc camera and mailing the film to West Germany, where it was forwarded to his "principals" in East Berlin. He also admitted carrying some film personally to East Berlin. On a visit to East Germany in November 1975, he was told to get a position in the U.S. government that would give him access to classified information. That's what he was trying to do when his cover was blown.

The story ends with some mysterious loose ends. How did the FBI learn about him before he applied for the House job? Why wasn't he prosecuted? Where is he today?

This is only one example of the complicated cases U.S. counterintelligence agents must deal with, at a time when the growing forces of the KGB are straining the resources of the U.S. agencies responsible for keeping watch on foreign spies.

APPENDIX C

Chronology of Intelligence Developments

1947
July 26 — National Security Act enacted, establishing National Security Council (NSC), Director of Central Intelligence (DCI), and Central Intelligence Agency (CIA).

1952
Nov. 4 — National Security Agency (NSA) established by presidential directive.

1961
Aug. 1 — Defense Intelligence Agency (DIA) established by Defense Department directive.

1973
Mar. 20 — Senate Foreign Relations subcommittee, headed by Sen. Frank Church, began hearings on ITT, CIA, and Chile.

1974
Sept. 8 — *New York Times* reported CIA activities in Chile under Allende regime; some acknowledged by President Ford Sept. 16.

Oct. 2 — Senate passed Hughes Amendment to Foreign Assistance Act. House passed similar amendment, sponsored by Rep. Leo Ryan, the following week. Differences resolved Dec. 17.

Dec. 9, 10 — Senate Government Relations Committee held hearings on Mansfield-Mathias resolution to create "Select Committee to Study Governmental Operations with Respect to Intelligence Activities."

Dec. 22 — First of a series of *New York Times* articles by Seymour Hersh alleged illegal CIA activities in the U.S. President Ford ordered investigations.

Dec. 30 — Hughes-Ryan Amendment became law.

1975
Jan. 5 — President Ford established President's Commission on CIA Activities Within the United States, chaired by Vice-President

	Nelson Rockefeller (commission became known as Rockefeller Commission).
Jan. 15	DCI Colby testified before Senate Appropriations subcommittee that questionable CIA domestic operations ceased Feb. 1973.
Jan. 27	Senate passed S. Res. 21 (94th Cong.), establishing Senate Select Committee to Study Government Operations with Respect to Intelligence Activities, chaired by Sen. Frank Church (committee became known as Church Committee).
Feb. 19	House passed H.Res. 139 (94th Cong.), establishing House Select Committee on Intelligence, chaired by Rep. Lucien Nedzi.
June 6	Rockefeller Commission submitted report to President Ford.
June 10	Rockefeller Commission Report released. Found that "the great majority" of CIA domestic activities were within the law but some were "plainly unlawful."
June 17	House Select Committee on Intelligence reconstituted by H.Res. 591 (94th Cong.) after internal turmoil. Rep. Otis Pike named chairman (committee became known as Pike Committee).
Nov. 14	Pike Committee voted contempt-of-Congress citations against Secretary Kissinger related to subpoenaed material on covert activities and Soviet compliance with SALT I. Accommodation was reached and citations were dropped on Dec. 2 and 10.
Nov. 20	Church Committee released report *Alleged Assassination Plots Involving Foreign Leaders*.
Dec. 4	Church Committee released report *Covert Action in Chile, 1963-1973*.
Dec. 19	Senate adopted amendment by Sen. John Tunney to deny funds to Angolan guerrillas.
Dec. 23	Richard S. Welsh, CIA station chief in Greece, assassinated.
1976	
Jan. 29	House of Representatives voted not to release Pike Committee's final report until the President certified that release would not harm intelligence activities abroad.
Feb. 16	Part of classified draft Pike Committee report published in the *Village Voice*; additional extracts published Feb. 23. CBS correspondent Daniel Schorr subsequently admitted giving report to the *Voice*.

1976 *(continued)*

Feb 18	President Ford issued Executive Order 11905 reorganizing U.S. intelligence.
Feb. 19	House passed H.Res. 1042 (94th Cong.), authorizing House Committee on Standards of Official Conduct to investigate publication of classified Pike Committee report.
Mar. 1	Senate Government Operations Committee favorably reported out S.Res. 400 (94th Cong.), to create standing Senate Committee on Intelligence.
Apr. 26	Church Committee released Book I, *Final Report, Foreign and Military Intelligence*.
Apr. 28	Church Committee released Book II, *Final Report, Intelligence Activities and the Rights of Americans*. It charged poor oversight had led to violations of constitutional rights.
May 19	Amended version of S.Res. 400 (94th Cong.) passed Senate, establishing Select Committee on Intelligence to oversee intelligence activities, with exclusive jurisdiction over DCI and CIA and shared jurisdiction over DIA, NSA, FBI, and State Department intelligence. Senator Daniel Inouye named chairman May 27.
Dec. 23	President-elect Carter announced nomination of Theodore Sorensen as DCI.

1977

Jan. 17	Sorensen withdrew his nomination in the face of growing opposition.
Feb. 7	Admiral Stansfield Turner nominated DCI; took office Mar. 9.
Mar. 11	Secretary of Defense Harold Brown reorganized Defense intelligence, combining it with Communications, Command, and Control, and having DIA and NSA report to Deputy Secretary of Defense.
May 5	President Carter named three-member Intelligence Oversight Board and abolished President's Foreign Intelligence Advisory Board (group of outside advisors on intelligence created by President Eisenhower in 1955).
May 16	S.1539 (95th Cong.), first public budget authorization for intelligence, introduced; disclosure limited to Intelligence Community Staff and CIA Retirement and Disability System.
July 14	House passed H.Res. 658 (95th Cong.) creating House Intelligence Committee. Rep. Edward Boland named chairman.

Aug. 4	President Carter announced further reorganization of intelligence, again strengthening role of DCI. Changes codified in Executive Order 12036, Jan. 24, 1978 (see below).
Aug. 9	DCI Turner announced planned reduction of CIA's Directorate of Operations (DDO) by 800 positions.
Oct. 11	CIA's Directorate of Intelligence (DDI) redesignated National Foreign Assessment Center (NFAC).
Oct. 31	Former DCI Richard Helms pleaded "no contest" to two charges of failing to testify fully and accurately on operations in Chile before Senate Foreign Relations Committee in 1973.
Dec. 2	CIA announced "voluntarily imposed" guidelines on relations with U.S. journalists and news media.
1978	
Jan. 24	President Carter issued Executive Order 12036, confirming central role of DCI in setting priorities for intelligence budget; setting up organizations to assist DCI; defining functions and responsibilities of each Intelligence Community component; restricting certain collection techniques and questionable activities; and providing further improvements in executive oversight.
Feb. 9	S.2525 (95th Cong.), draft Intelligence Charter, introduced.
Apr. 20	House Intelligence Committee voted against disclosing intelligence funds it had authorized for fiscal year 1979.
	Senate passed S.1566 (95th Cong.), Foreign Intelligence Surveillance Act.
Sept. 7	House passed H.R. 7308 (95th Cong.), its version of Foreign Intelligence Surveillance Act. Differences resolved in conference.
Oct. 25	Foreign Intelligence Surveillance Act became law.
Nov. 11	President Carter reportedly sent memorandum to DCI Turner, Secretary of State Cyrus Vance, and National Security Assistant Zbigniew Brzezinski expressing dissatisfaction with quality of political intelligence he was receiving.
Nov. 18	Former CIA employee William P. Kampiles convicted of espionage in sale of KH-11 satellite manual to Soviet Union.

Notes

Chapter One

1. Alexis de Tocqueville, *Democracy in America* (New York: Knopf, 1945), vol. I, pp. 234–35.
2. *Washington Post,* February 5, 1979.
3. *Washington Post,* February 26, 1979.
4. *Washington Star,* March 9, 1979.
5. *Washington Post,* March 1, 1979.
6. *New York Times,* March 12, 1979.
7. See Robert Moss, "The Campaign to Destabilise Iran," *Conflict Studies* No. 101 (November 1978).
8. Cord Meyer, "The Kremlin's Work in Iran," *Washington Star,* February 10, 1979.
9. Cited in *ibid.*
10. U.S. Senate, Select Committee to Study Governmental Operations with Respect to Intelligence Activities, *Final Report,* Book I, 1976, pp. 163 ff. Director Webster's address was delivered in Chicago, October 26, 1978.
11. Melvin R. Laird, "Why We Need Spies," *Reader's Digest,* March 1979, p. 87.
12. Abraham Lincoln's debate, Ottawa, Illinois, August 21, 1858.
13. From a statement by William E. Colby, director of central intelligence, submitted to the Senate Appropriations Committee, January 15, 1975; *New York Times,* January 16, 1975.
14. Paul Ramsey, *The Just War: Force and Political Responsibility* (New York: Scribner's, 1968), p. xi; see also pp. vii–xvii and 178–88. See also Robert W. Tucker, *The Just War: A Study in Contemporary Doctrine* (Baltimore: Johns Hopkins Press, 1960).
15. It should be noted that all societies and political philosophies have their own "just war" theories. For Mussolini and Hitler, wars of territorial expansion were justified. For the Communists, revolutionary wars and "wars of national liberation" are just. "There are wars," said V. I. Lenin, "which are just and unjust, progressive and reactionary, wars of the leading classes and wars of the backward classes, wars which serve to strengthen class oppression and wars which are aimed at overthrowing it" (*Complete Works of Lenin,* vol. 38, p. 337).

Chapter Two

1. Interview with George Cary, CIA legislative counsel 1974-78.
2. Mitchell Rogovin, special counsel to the director of central intelligence; in U.S. House of Representatives, Select Committee on Intelligence,

Hearings, December 9, 1975, p. 1737. (Cited hereafter as the Pike Committee.)

3. U.S. Senate, Select Committee to Study Governmental Operations with Respect to Intelligence Activities, *Final Report,* Book I, 1976, p. 508. (Cited hereafter as the Church Committee.)

4. David Wise, "Is Anybody Watching the CIA?," *Inquiry,* November 27, 1978, p. 18.

5. *Ibid.,* p. 19.

6. See, for example, the testimony of former senior officials who testified against similar provisions in the proposed Charter for the CIA; U.S. Senate, Committee on Intelligence, *Hearings on the National Intelligence Reorganization and Reform Act of 1978,* 95th Congress, Second Session, 1978. (Cited hereafter as the Senate Intelligence Committee.)

7. Former CIA director William Colby has written that "every" new project subjected to the procedure of Hughes-Ryan in 1975 was leaked; *Honorable Men* (New York: Simon and Schuster, 1978), p. 423.

8. U.S. House, Permanent Select Committee on Intelligence, *Hearings on Foreign Intelligence, Electronic Surveillance,* 95th Congress, Second Session, 1978, pp. 13–66. (The House Permanent Committee created in 1977 will be referred to hereafter as the House Intelligence Committee.) See also *Congressional Record,* September 7, 1978, p. H9259, and October 12, 1978, p. H12539.

9. *Congressional Record,* October 12, 1978, p. H12541.

10. "Intelligence Charter Debate to Focus on Civil Liberties, National Security Conflicts," *Congressional Quarterly,* December 23, 1978, pp. 3741–46.

11. Senate Intelligence Committee, *Hearings on the National Intelligence Reorganization and Reform Act of 1978,* p. v.

12. *Ibid.,* p. 308. In this article, the quotation is from the original text of the AFIO statement as submitted to the Senate. In the *Hearings* record, this original text is garbled beyond comprehension.

13. For a description of congressional oversight from the creation of the CIA until the early 1970s, see Harry Howe Ransom, "Congress and the Intelligence Agencies," in Harvey Mansfield, ed., *Congress and the Presidency, Annals,* vol. 32, no. 1, pp. 154–65. The following description is taken largely from this account.

14. Church Committee, *Final Report,* Book I, p. 3.

15. *Ibid.,* p. 7.

16. *Ibid.*

17. *Ibid.,* p. 8.

18. For the legislative history of S.Res. 400 creating the Senate Intelligence Committee, see William Newby Raiford, "To Create a Senate Select Committee on Intelligence," Congressional Research Service, Library of Congress, August 12, 1976.

19. For brief descriptions of House activities with respect to the intelli-

gence agencies and oversight, see the Issue Briefs prepared periodically by Congressional Research Service, particularly "Intelligence Community: Congressional Oversight," which has been updated and published periodically since 1976.

20. Interview with Spencer Davis.
21. Senate Intelligence Committee, *Annual Report,* May 18, 1977.
22. House Intelligence Committee, *Annual Report,* October 14, 1978, p. 1.
23. See, for example, Morris Ogul, *Congress Oversees the Bureaucracy* (Pittsburgh: University of Pittsburgh Press, 1977); Lawrence Dodd and Bruce Oppenheim, *Congress Reconsidered* (New York: Praeger, 1977).
24. For a description of the House Committee's activities with respect to performance and evaluation, see the previously cited *Annual Report.*
25. House Intelligence Committee, *Annual Report,* p. 16.
26. See the *Annual Reports* and, for example, the "Report to the Senate on the Work of the Senate Select Committee on Intelligence" by its first chairman, Senator Daniel K. Inouye, Senate Intelligence Committee, 1977. See also Wise, "Is Anybody Watching the CIA?"
27. Senate Intelligence Committee, "Activities of 'Friendly' Foreign Intelligence Services in the United States: A Case Study," June 1978, p. 2.
28. Wise, "Is Anybody Watching the CIA?," p. 19.
29. Church Committee, *Final Report,* Book I, p. III. Emphasis added.
30. Pike Committee, "U.S. Intelligence Agencies and Activities: Intelligence Costs and Fiscal Procedures," July-August 1975, pp. 1-2.
31. *CIA: The Pike Report* (Nottingham, England: Spokesman Books, 1977). It is this edition which is cited in this article.
32. Church Committee, *Final Report,* Book I, p. 257.
33. *Ibid.,* p. 54.
34. Senate Intelligence Committee, "The National Intelligence Estimates—A-B Team Episode Concerning Soviet Strategic Capability and Objectives," February 16, 1978, p. 5.
35. Interview with Davis.
36. Unfortunately, while the committee apparently believes that the intelligence agencies should provide the public with information about their inner workings under the Freedom of Information Act, it subscribes to a different set of standards for itself. In response to a request to study the unclassified papers of the Church Committee and its successor, the Senate Intelligence Committee, this writer was informed by the current chairman of the Senate Intelligence Committee that *all* the papers and files of both committees were "classified" and that it was not possible for an outside scholar to review them at this time. Letter from Senator Birch Bayh, March 30, 1979.
37. Interview with Joseph Trento.
38. *Ibid.*
39. *Ibid.*
40. Interview with Davis.
41. Interview with Trento.

Chapter Three

1. Morton Halperin, Jerry Berman, Robert Borosage, and Christine Marwick, *The Lawless State* (New York: Penguin Books, 1976), p. 5.
2. *Ibid.*, p. 6.
3. Richard J. Barnet, *The Economy of Death* (New York: Atheneum, 1969), p. 42.
4. Richard J. Barnet, "The 'Dirty Tricks' Gap," in Robert C. Borosage and John Marks, eds., *The CIA File* (New York: Grossman, 1976), p. 218.
5. U.S. Senate, Select Committee on Intelligence, *Hearings on the National Intelligence Reorganization and Reform Act of 1978*, April, June, July, August, 1978, 95th Congress, 2nd Session, 1978, p. 581.
6. Barnet, "The 'Dirty Tricks' Gap," pp. 218–19.
7. See, for example, "CIA's Covert Operations Vs. Human Rights," Center for National Security Studies, 1977.
8. An internal opposition group in the NLG, the Democratic Caucus, has complained a good deal about the NLG leadership and particularly its International Committee, which it claims has identified the guild "with the politics of the 'socialist' countries on every major issue" and has conducted "Guild affairs as though we were a committed Marxist-Leninist entity." See Documents of the NLG Democratic Caucus, *Congressional Record*, March 3, 1978, pp. E1021-27. On the NLG's finances, see *Guild Notes*, Dec. 1973.
9. ACLU, *Annual Report*, 1970-1971, p. 23.
10. ACLU Foundation, Financial Report 1977, Special Projects: National Security, $199,243, as reported in *Civil Liberties*, November 1978, p. 7.
11. "Beginning the Second Decade, 1963-1973," Institute for Policy Studies, 1974.
12. "The Samuel Rubin Foundation" Internal Revenue Service Form 990, 1975-1977, indicates that approximately half of the IPS budget was derived from this foundation. According to the *Washington Post*, January 23, 1977, the total annual budget of IPS is approximately $1 million.
13. U.S. Senate, Committee on the Judiciary, Internal Security Subcommittee, *Hearings on Subversion of Law Enforcement by Intelligence Gathering Operations*, Part I, Organizing Committee for a Fifth Estate, March 26, 1976, 94th Congress, 2nd session, 1976, p. 33.
14. *Washington Post*, August 3, 1978; August 4, 1978.
15. "Background," three mimeographed pages distributed at CNSS conference on "The CIA and Covert Action" at Dirksen Senate Office Building, September 12–13, 1974.
16. These objectives are stated both explicitly and implicitly in the center's publications. The center in 1977, for example, supported H.R. 6051, which would, as the center put it, not only ban all covert action and espionage but also "dismantle the CIA's clandestine services completely" ("CIA's Covert Operations Vs. Human Rights").

17. Center for National Security Studies, "Intern Program" (undated).
18. "The Center for National Security Studies: Activities, Publications, Library, Litigation" (undated).
19. Interview with Morton Halperin.
20. "The Fund for Peace: Issues of Survival in the Modern World" (undated).
21. National Organizing Conference to Stop Government Spying, "Conference Report," 1978, p. 6.
22. For example, there have been some 20–25 articles and books in English alone alleging that senior U.S. trade union officials have been CIA agents of one kind or another. Almost all the publications cite as their source publications of other authors. Only two, Philip Agee and Tom Braden, claim firsthand knowledge of this relationship. They are cited again and again. So far, no one has produced any substantial documentary evidence. For a list of the major books and articles on this alleged relationship, see "American Labor and World Affairs: A Bibliography," International Labor Program, Papers No. 2, Georgetown University, Washington, D.C., 1978.
23. U.S. House of Representatives, Permanent Select Committee on Intelligence, *Hearings on the CIA and the Media,* 95th Congress, 2nd session, 1978, p. 188.
24. *Treason* (quarterly publication of the Free University of New York), Summer 1967, p. 18.
25. *Guardian,* November 30, 1968, p. 8.
26. Philip Agee, *Inside the Company: CIA Diary* (London: Penguin, 1975), pp. 639–40.
27. For example, Philip Agee and Louis Wolf's *Dirty Work: The CIA in Western Europe* (New York: Lyle Stuart, 1978) lists nearly 300 pages of names and addresses of alleged CIA employees.
28. U.S. Senate, Committee on Government Operations, *Hearings on Legislative Proposals to Strengthen Congressional Oversight of the Nation's Intelligence Agencies,* December 1974, 93rd Congress, 2nd session, 1975, pp. 22–25.
29. Center for International Policy, "International Policy Report," September 1976, p. 20. The same paper lists David Aaron as a consultant to the organization. Aaron was then also a senior member of the staff of the Church Committee and later of its successor, until he became a senior staff member of the National Security Council in 1977. Aaron now reportedly is the NSC official responsible for intelligence reform.
30. U.S. Senate, Committee on Government Operations, *Hearings on Legislative Proposals to Strengthen Congressional Oversight.*
31. Morton Halperin and Jeremy Stone, "Secrecy and Covert Intelligence Collection and Operations," in Norman Dorsen and Stephen Gillers, eds., *None of Your Business* (New York: Viking Press, 1974), pp. 105–36.
32. See, for example, "Paper Trail: Notes on the Center for National Secu-

rity Studies, Activities Summer, 1977" and "Activities Report," January 1-September 30, 1978.

33. Victor Marchetti and John Marks, *The CIA and the Cult of Intelligence* (New York: Knopf, 1974), p. xv.

34. "Beginning the Second Decade, 1963-1973," Institute for Policy Studies, 1974, p. 2.

35. Robert C. Borosage and John Marks, eds., *The CIA File*, p. vii.

36. See, for example, the ACLU Reports, especially "The Politics of Rights: Civil Liberties in the 95th Congress," 1979.

37. U.S. Senate, Select Committee on Intelligence, *Hearings on the Nomination of Ambassador Frank C. Carlucci*, January 1978, 95th Congress, 2nd session, 1978, p. 35.

38. *Congressional Record*, Senate, April 20, 1978, p. S6018.

39. *Congressional Record*, House, September 7, 1978, p. H9259.

40. *Congressional Record*, House, October 12, 1978, p. H12534.

41. See, for example, Robert Cox, "Labor and Hegemony," in *International Organization*, Summer 1977, especially p. 396.

42. See, for example, the remarks of former DCIs Bush, Colby, and Helms in "CIA Roundtable," *The Washington Quarterly*, Autumn 1978, pp. 34-35. For similar conclusions, see the remarks by President Ford and DCI James Schlesinger in the *New York Times*, August 3 and 4, 1975, and the *Washington Post*, August 3, 1975. For an even more specific discussion of the perception of foreigners about U.S. disclosure, see "Statement of Frank C. Carlucci, Deputy Director of the CIA, Before the House Permanent Select Committee on Intelligence, April 5, 1979." Many newspaper and news magazine stories from 1975 through 1978 also quote identified and unidentified CIA sources as indicating that investigations, disclosures, and leaks were drying up foreign sources and damaging agency morale. For example, *Time*, August 4, 1975, pp. 9-10; *Washington Post*, November 9, 1975, and January 17, 1976.

43. *Ibid.*

44. See, for example, David Philips, *The Night Watch* (New York: Atheneum, 1977), pp. 261-62, 287-88.

45. On the origin of AFIO, see *ibid.*, pp. 271, 285-86. On the growth and activities of the organization, see AFIO's brochure "AFIO: Association of Intelligence Professionals" and the bimonthly newsletter *Periscope*. The following account is drawn largely from these sources and from interviews with AFIO officials in the spring of 1979.

46. See "An AFIO Statement on Reduction of Personnel at CIA," *Periscope*, vol. IV, no. 1, 1978, p. 8, and a critical article in *CIRA Newsletter*, vol. III, no. 1, 1978, pp. 18-20. CIRA, the Central Intelligence Retiree Association, is open only to former employees of the CIA.

47. *CIRA Newsletter*, vol. III, no. 4, pp. 19-20.

48. Fund-raising letter signed by James Angleton, Elbridge Durbrow, and Robert C. Richardson, Security and Intelligence Fund, July 10, 1978.

49. Fund-raising letter signed by Angleton, Durbrow, and Richardson, Security and Intelligence Fund (undated).

Chapter Four

1. Robert T. Bower, *Television and the Public* (New York: Holt, Rinehart, and Winston, 1973), p. 99. For details on the national news viewing audience, see "The News on Television," pp. 99–123.
2. Edward Jay Epstein, "The Strange Tilted World of TV Network News," *Reader's Digest*, February 1974, p. 17. See also Epstein's *News from Nowhere: Television and the News* (New York: Random House, 1973), pp. 64–73.
3. FCC 74–702 (18425), released July 12, 1974.
4. For a brief discussion of the Fairness Doctrine see Ernest W. Lefever, *TV and National Defense: An Analysis of CBS News, 1972-1973* (Boston, Virginia: Institute for American Strategy, 1974), pp. 4–9.
5. Lefever, *TV and National Defense;* see especially "Patterns and Themes of CBS News," pp. 24–46.
6. Commission on CIA Activities within the United States, *Report to the President*, June 1975. Vice-President Nelson Rockefeller was chairman of the commission.
7. A considerable volume of information available in the United States about political developments in Chile during the Allende period (congressional hearings, published articles, and a chronology and bibliography prepared by the Library of Congress) was assembled and published in U.S. House, Committee on Foreign Affairs, Subcommittee on Inter-American Affairs, *United States and Chile During the Allende Years, 1970-1973*, 93rd Congress, 2nd Session, 1975. Virtually all this material was in the public domain before September 1974. Although a relatively small portion of the 677 pages deals with the role of the Soviet Union and Cuba in Chile, there is ample evidence of external Soviet and Cuban activity. Among the contributors who provide testimony on external Communist activity in the country are: Ambassador Edward M. Korry, July 1, 1971 (pp. 2–31); Paul F. Wallner and Lt. Nelson H. Litsinger, U.S.N., both of the Defense Intelligence Agency, October 31, 1973 (pp. 159–65); Dr. Ernest W. Lefever, who based his statement on an eleven-day investigation in Chile, July 1-11, 1974, with Dr. Riordan Roett, director of Latin American studies at Johns Hopkins University, and Dr. Albert Blaustein of the Rutgers University Law School, August 5, 1974 (pp. 181–220); and Dr. James D. Theberge, then director of Latin American studies, Center for Strategic and International Studies of Georgetown University, September 17, 1974 (pp. 309–24).
8. *Code of Broadcast News Ethics,* Radio and Television News Directors Association, adopted January 1966, amended October 1973. See Articles 1 and 2.

Bibliography

GENERAL WORKS

Agee, Philip. *Inside the Company: CIA Diary*. Ontario, Canada: Penguin Books, 1975.

──── , and Louis Wolf. *Dirty Work: The CIA in Western Europe*. New York: Lyle Stuart, 1978.

Barnds, William J. "Intelligence and Foreign Policy: Dilemmas of a Democracy." *Foreign Affairs,* January 1969.

Barnet, Richard J. *The Economy of Death*. New York: Atheneum, 1969.

Barron, John. *KGB: The Work of Soviet Secret Agents*. New York: Reader's Digest Press, 1974.

Blackstock, Paul W., and Frank L. Schaf, Jr., eds. *Intelligence, Espionage, Counterespionage, and Covert Operations: A Guide to Information Sources*. Detroit: Gale Research Company, 1978.

Blum, Richard H., ed. *Surveillance and Espionage in a Free Society. A Report by the Planning Group on Intelligence and Security to the Policy Council of the Democratic National Committee*. New York: Praeger, 1972.

Borosage, Robert C., and John Marks, eds. *The CIA File*. New York: Grossman, 1976.

Bower, Robert T. *Television and the Public*. New York: Holt, Rinehart, and Winston, 1973.

Center for National Security Studies. *CIA's Covert Operations Vs. Human Rights*. Washington, D.C.: Center for National Security Studies, 1977.

Cline, Ray S. *Secrets, Spies, and Scholars*. Washington: Acropolis Books, 1976.

Colby, William. *Honorable Men*. New York: Simon and Schuster, 1978.

Copeland, Miles. *Without Cloak or Dagger*. New York: Simon and Schuster, 1978.

Dodd, Lawrence, and Bruce Oppenheim. *Congress Reconsidered*. New York: Praeger, 1977.

Dorsen, Norman, and Stephan Gillers, eds. *None of Your Business*. New York: Viking Press, 1974.

Dulles, Allen W. *The Craft of Intelligence*. New York: Harper and Row, 1963.

Epstein, Edward Jay. *News From Nowhere: Television and the News.* New York: Random House, 1973.

Fain, Tyrus, ed. *The Intelligence Community.* New York: R. R. Bowker, 1977.

Franck, Thomas M., and Edward Weisband, eds. *Secrecy and Foreign Policy.* New York: Oxford University Press, 1974.

Godson, Roy, ed. *Intelligence Requirements for the 1980's: Elements of Intelligence.* Washington, D.C.: National Strategy Information Center, 1979.

Graham, Daniel O. *U.S. Intelligence at the Crossroads.* Washington, D.C.: United States Strategic Institute, 1976.

Halperin, Morton H., Jerry Berman, Robert L. Borosage, and Christine M. Marwick. *The Lawless State–The Crimes of the U.S. Intelligence Agencies.* New York: Penguin Books, 1976.

Katzenbach, Nicholas deB. "Foreign Policy, Public Opinion and Secrecy." *Foreign Affairs,* October 1973.

Kirkpatrick, Lyman B., Jr. *The Real CIA.* New York: Macmillan, 1968.

———. *The U.S. Intelligence Community.* New York: Hill and Wang, 1973.

Lefever, Ernest W. "The CIA and American Foreign Policy." *Lugano Review,* 1975, 4.

———. *TV and National Defense: An Analysis of CBS News, 1972-1973.* Boston, Virginia: Institute for American Strategy, 1974.

Loory, Stuart H. "The CIA's Use of the Press: A 'Mighty Wurlitzer.'" *Columbia Journalism Review,* September/October 1974.

Marchetti, Victor, and John D. Marks. *The CIA and the Cult of Intelligence.* New York: Knopf, 1974.

Moss, Robert. "The Campaign to Destabilise Iran." *Conflict Studies* No. 101 (November 1978).

Murphy, Charles J. V. "Uncloaking the CIA." *Fortune,* June 1975.

Ogul, Morris. *Congress Oversees the Bureaucracy.* Pittsburgh: University of Pittsburgh Press, 1977.

Philips, David. *The Night Watch.* New York: Atheneum, 1977.

Powers, Thomas. *The Man Who Kept the Secrets: Richard Helms and the CIA.* New York: Knopf, 1979.

Ramsey, Paul. *The Just War: Force and Political Responsibility.* New York: Scribner's, 1968.

Ransom, Harry Howe. *Central Intelligence and National Security.* Cambridge, Massachusetts: Harvard University Press, 1958.

———. *The Intelligence Establishment.* Cambridge, Massachusetts: Harvard University Press, 1970.

_____. *Strategic Intelligence*. Morristown, New Jersey: General Learning Press, 1973.

Tucker, Robert W. *The Just War: A Study in Contemporary Doctrine*. Baltimore: Johns Hopkins Press, 1960.

Wise, David, and Thomas B. Ross. *The Espionage Establishment*. New York: Random House, 1967.

U.S. GOVERNMENT DOCUMENTS

Commission on CIA Activities Within the U.S. (Rockefeller Commission). *Report to the President on CIA Activities Within the U.S.* Washington: G.P.O., 1975.

House of Representatives

Committee on Foreign Affairs, Subcommittee on Inter-American Affairs. *United States and Chile During the Allende Years, 1970-73*. Hearings, 92d Cong., 1st and 2d sess. Washington: G.P.O., 1975.

Committee on Standards of Official Conduct. *Investigation of Publication of Select Committee on Intelligence Report*. Hearings, 94th Cong., 2d sess. Washington: G.P.O., 1976.

_____. *Report on the Investigation Pursuant to H.Res. 1042 Concerning Unauthorized Publication of the Report of the Select Committee on Intelligence*. 94th Cong., 2d sess., H.Rept. 94-1754. Washington: G.P.O., 1976.

Permanent Select Committee on Intelligence. *Annual Report*. 95th Cong., 2d sess., H.Rept. 95-1795. Washington: G.P.O., 1978.

_____. *The CIA and the Media*. Hearings, 95th Cong., 1st and 2d sess. Washington: G.P.O., 1978.

_____. *Disclosure of Funds for Intelligence Activities*. Hearings, 95th Cong., 2d sess. Washington: G.P.O., 1978.

_____. *Foreign Intelligence Electronic Surveillance*. Hearings, 95th Cong., 2d sess., on H.R. 7308. Washington: G.P.O., 1978.

_____. *Iran: Evaluation of U.S. Intelligence Performance Prior to November 1978*. Committee Print, 95th Cong., 2d sess. Washington: G.P.O., 1979.

Select Committee on Intelligence. *Recommendations of the Final Report*. 94th Cong., 2d sess., H.Rept. 94-833. Washington: G.P.O., 1976.

_____. *U.S. Intelligence Agencies and Activities* (Part 1—Intelligence Costs and Financial Procedures, Part 2—The Performance of the Intelligence Community, Part 3—Domestic Intelligence Programs, Part 4—Committee Proceedings—I, Part 5—Risks and Control of Foreign Intelligence, Part 6—Committee Proceedings—II). Hearings, 94th Cong., 1st and 2d sess. Washington: G.P.O., 1975-76.

Library of Congress. Congressional Research Service

American Law Division. *Legislative History of the Central Intelligence Agency as Documented in Published Congressional Sources* [by] Grover S. Williams. CRS Report 75–5A. Washington, 1975.

Foreign Affairs and National Defense Division. *The Central Intelligence Agency: Organizational History* [by] Mark M. Lowenthal. CRS Report 78-168F. Washington, 1978.

———. *To Create a Senate Select Committee on Intelligence: A Legislative History* [by] William N. Raiford. CRS Report 76-149F. Washington, 1976.

———. *Intelligence Community: Congressional Oversight* [by] Mark M. Lowenthal. Issue Brief 77079. Washington, 1977 (continuously updated).

———. *Intelligence Community Investigation* [by] Richard F. Grimmett. Archived Issue Brief 75037. Washington, 1975.

———. *Intelligence Community: Reform and Reorganization* [by] Mark M. Lowenthal. Issue Brief 76039. Washington, 1976 (continuously updated).

———. *The National Security Council: Organizational History* [by] Mark M. Lowenthal. CRS Report 78-104F. Washington, 1978.

———. *The President's Foreign Intelligence Advisory Board: An Historical and Contemporary Analysis (1955-1975)* [by] John Steven Chwat. CRS Report 75-225F. Washington, 1975.

Senate

Committee on Government Operations. *Hearings on Legislative Proposals to Strengthen Congressional Oversight of the Nation's Intelligence Agencies.* 93rd Cong., 2d sess. Washington: G.P.O., 1975.

———. *Oversight of U.S. Government Intelligence Function.* Hearings, 94th Cong., 2d sess., on S.Con.Res. 4, S. 2893, and S. 2865. Washington: G.P.O., 1976.

Committee on the Judiciary, Internal Security Subcommittee. *Hearings on Subversion of Law Enforcement by Intelligence Gathering Operations.* 94th Cong., 1st sess., S.Rept. 94-465. Washington: G.P.O., 1975.

Select Committee on Intelligence. *Activities of "Friendly" Intelligence Services in the U.S.: A Case Study.* Committee Print, 95th Cong., 2d sess. Washington: G.P.O., 1978.

———. *Annual Report to the Senate.* 95th Cong., 1st sess., S.Rept. 95-217. Washington: G.P.O., 1977.

———. *Foreign Intelligence Surveillance Act of 1978.* Hearings, 95th Cong., 2d sess., on S. 1566. Washington: G.P.O., 1978.

BIBLIOGRAPHY 157

———. *The National Intelligence A-B Team Episode Concerning Soviet Strategic Capability and Objectives.* Committee Print, 95th Cong., 2d sess. Washington: G.P.O., 1978.

———. *National Intelligence Reorganization and Reform Act of 1978.* Hearings, 95th cong., 2d sess., on S. 2525. Washington: G.P.O., 1978.

———. *Report to the Senate, Covering the Period May 16, 1977, to December 31, 1978.* 96th Cong., 1st sess., S.Rept. 96-141. Washington: G.P.O., 1979.

———. *The Soviet Oil Situation: An Evaluation of CIA Analyses of Soviet Oil Production.* Committee Print, 95th Cong., 2d sess. Washington: G.P.O., 1977.

———. *U.S. Intelligence and the Oil Issue, 1973-1974.* Committee Print, 95th Cong., 2d sess. Washington: G.P.O., 1977.

———. *Whether Disclosure of Funds Authorized for Intelligence Activities Is in the Public Interest.* Hearings, 95th Cong., 1st and 2d sess., S.Rept. 95-274. Washington: G.P.O., 1977.

Select Committee to Study Governmental Operations with Respect to Intelligence Activities. *Alleged Assassination Plots Concerning Foreign Leaders.* 94th Cong., 1st sess., S. Rept. 94-465. Washington: G.P.O., 1975.

———. *Covert Action in Chile, 1963-1973.* Staff Report, 94th Cong., 1st sess. Washington: G.P.O., 1975.

———. *Final Report* (Book I—Foreign and Military Intelligence, Book II—Intelligence Activities and the Rights of Americans, Book III—Supplementary Detailed Staff Reports on Intelligence Activities and the Rights of Americans, Book IV—Supplementary Detailed Staff Reports on Foreign and Military Intelligence, Book V—The Investigation of the Assassination of President John F. Kennedy: Performance of the Intelligence Agencies, Book VI—Supplementary Reports on Intelligence Activities). 94th Cong., 2d sess., S.Rept. 94-755. Washington: G.P.O., 1976.

———. *Hearings* (v. 1—Unauthorized Storage of Toxic Agents, v. 2—Huston Plan, v. 3—Internal Revenue Service, v. 4—Mail Openings, v. 5—The National Security Agency and Fourth Amendment Rights, v. 6—The Federal Bureau of Investigation, v. 7—Covert Action). Hearings, 94th Cong., 1st sess. Washington: G.P.O., 1976.

Index of Names

Acheson, Dean, 12
Afghanistan, 5
Agee, Philip, 76, 81-82, 89
Agency for International Development (AID), 79
Allende, President Salvadore, 114-16
Alperovitz, Gar, 74
American Broadcasting Company (ABC), 11, 97-98, 111-12, 118
American Civil Liberties Union (ACLU), 30, 32, 70, 72-74, 84-88
American Security Council, 93
Americans for Democratic Action (ADA), 87
Angleton, James, 94
Angola, 21, 27, 99
Ashbrook, Rep. John, 47
Aspin, Rep. Les, 26, 47
Association of Former Intelligence Officers (AFIO), 29, 33, 91-93
Athens, 105

Baader-Meinhoff gang, 72
Barnet, Richard, 70, 74
Bayh, Sen. Birch, 26, 45
Berle, Adolf, 72
Bork, Robert, 94
Borosage, Robert, 75, 85
Braden, Tom, 89
Brezhnev, Chairman Leonid, 4
Brooke, Sen. Edward, 77
Brookings Institution, 84
Bush, George, 94

Campaign for Political Rights, 74, 78
Carter, President Jimmy, 2, 4, 26, 40, 58, 88
Case, Sen. Clifford, 85
Castro, Fidel, 54
Center for Defense Information, 78
Center for International Policy, 78, 83
Center for National Security Studies (CNSS), 30, 32, 74, 76-78, 84-87
Central Intelligence Retiree Association, 93

Chancellor, John, 115
Chile, 23, 34, 54, 63, 70, 89, 99, 101-2, 105, 113-16; Chilean Secret Service, 100
China, People's Republic of, 9, 100
China, Republic of, viii
Church, Sen. Frank, 10, 21, 60, 105, 115
Churchill, Winston, vii
Civil Rights Congress, 73
Code of Broadcast News Ethics, 118
Colby, William E., 12, 34, 53, 60, 85, 94, 115
Columbia Broadcasting System (CBS), 11, 97-98, 111-12, 117-18
Communist party U.S.A., 73
Cooper, Sen. John Sherman, 83
Counterspy, 73, 75-76, 78, 80-81, 89, 105
Counter-watch, 76, 80
Covert Action Information Bulletin, 76
Cuba, viii, 9, 71-72, 81, 115, 121; Cuban Communist party, 81
Cyprus, 24

Davis, Spencer, 40, 60-61, 63
Defense Intelligence Agency (DIA), 7, 109
diSuvero, Henry M., 73
DJB Foundation, 76
Donner, Frank J., 73

Ellsberg, Daniel, 72, 75
Emergency Civil Liberties Committee, 73

Fairness Doctrine, 97
Federal Bureau of Investigation (FBI), 6, 9, 10, 30-31, 37, 56, 88, 109
Field Foundation, 75, 78
Ford, President Gerald R., 26, 60, 88, 105, 115
Foreign Intelligence Surveillance Act (FISA), 28-30, 64, 80, 87-88, 94
Fund for Peace, 78, 84

160 INDEX OF NAMES

Germany, East (German Democratic Republic), 89
Gordon, Eda, 76
GRU (military arm of KGB), 4, 8

Halperin, Morton, 75, 77, 83-84, 87
Harrington, Rep. Michael, 34, 40, 98, 101
Hart, Sen. Philip, 77
Helms, Richard, 53, 94, 115
Hersh, Seymour, 26, 35, 63, 84, 98, 101
Hitler, Adolf, 15
Hue (Vietnam), 16
Hughes, Sen. Harold, 23
Hughes-Ryan Amendment, 23-27
Humphrey, Hubert, 89
Hussein, King (Jordan), 21

Indochina, 8
Institute for Policy Studies (IPS) 70, 74-75, 85
Institute for the Study of Conflict, 4
Intelligence Charter (draft), 30-33
Intelligence Documentation Center, 76
International Communications Agency (ICA), 79
International Telephone and Telegraph (ITT), 62
Iran, 2-5, 10, 59, 71, 121
Iraq, 21
Italy, 21

Jackson, Sen. Henry, 3
Jesus Christ, 17

Kampiles, William, 93
Kastenmeier, Rep. Robert, 88
Kennedy, Sen. Edward, 88
KGB (Soviet Committee for State Security), viii, 4, 8-9, 13, 20, 71, 109, 117, 132-39
Khomeini, Ayatollah, 3
Kissinger, Henry, 2, 10, 55, 84, 115
Korea, Republic of (South), viii, 71; South Korean CIA, 46, 100
Korean War, 83
Korry, Edward, 62

Laird, Melvin R., 10
Lincoln, Abraham, 11
Luce, Clare Boothe, 94

McCarthy, Eugene, 89
McCone, John, 54
Mailer, Norman, 75

Marchetti, Victor, 75, 83, 85
Mansfield, Sen. Mike, 35, 83
Marks, John, 83-85
Mathias, Sen. Charles, 35, 83
Miller, William G., 38, 61, 83-84
Mother Jones, 75
Moynihan, Sen. Daniel P., viii, 47
My Lai (Vietnam), 16

National Counter-Intelligence Corps Association, 93
National Broadcasting Company (NBC) 11, 97-98, 111-12, 117-18
National Emergency Civil Liberties Committee (NECLC), 72-73
National Lawyers Guild (NLG), 72, 76
National Reconnaissance Organization (NRO), 7
National Security Act, 36, 127-31
National Security Agency (NSA) 7, 29, 32, 88, 109
National Security Council (NSC), 11-12, 32, 36, 84
Nedzi, Rep. Lucien, 39
New York Times, 96-98, 116
Newsweek, 116
Nicaragua, 121
North American Council on Latin America (NACLA), 81
Novak, Robert, 63

O'Neill, Rep. Thomas P., 40
Organizing Committee for the Fifth Estate, 75

Palestine Liberation Organization (PLO), 72
Peace Corps, 79
Pearl Harbor, 8
Pike, Rep. Otis, 21, 39
Pipkin, George, 75
Poland, 15
Public Education Project on the Intelligence Community, 78

Radio Free Europe, 7, 53
Radio Liberty, 7, 53
Ramparts, 89
Ramsey, Paul (quoted), 14
Raskin, Marcus, 74-76, 83, 85
Ray, Ellen, 76
Rockefeller, Nelson, 105
Rockefeller Report, 60
Roosevelt, Theodore, 98
Russell, Sen. Richard, 33

INDEX OF NAMES

Ryan, Rep. Leo, 24

Safire, William, 63
SALT II treaty, 4
Samuel Rubin Foundation, 75
SAVAK (Iranian secret police), 4, 100
Schaap, William, 76
Schlesinger, James, 60
Schorr, Daniel, 40
Security and Intelligence Fund, 93
Shah of Iran, 4-5, 9, 59
Simon, William, 94
Stavins, Richard, 75
Stern Fund, 75
Students for a Democratic Society (SDS), 72, 81

Television News Index and Abstracts, 98-99, 101
Tet Offensive of 1968, 51
Time, 116, 125
Tocqueville, Alexis de, 2
Trento, Joseph, 62-63

Truman, President Harry S, 12
Turkey, 3
Turner, Stansfield, 2, 26

United Nations Charter, 15
United Nations Secretariat, 8

Veatch Program of the Unitarian Church, 78
Vietnam, 16, 19, 51, 72, 81
Vietnam Veterans Against the War, 75

Wall Street Journal, 125
Washington, George, 1
Washington Post, 116, 125
Waskow, Arthur, 74, 85
Watergate, 19, 99, 102
Webster, William, 9
Welsh, Richard, 105
World War II, 14, 17
Wright, Rep. Jim, 88

Yom Kippur War of 1973, 51

THE ETHICS AND PUBLIC POLICY CENTER, established at Georgetown University in 1976, affirms the moral validity and political relevance of the great Western ethical imperatives—respect for the human person, individual freedom, justice, the rule of law, and limited government. It also affirms the necessity for moral reasoning and empirical calculation in the discussing and deciding of public issues. The Center's program of research, writing, publication, and conferences is designed to encourage reflective debate on major domestic and foreign policy problems.

At the heart of the publication effort are original studies addressed to current issues, always against the backdrop of enduring concepts. To reach a broad academic and leadership audience these studies are written in lay language. The Center also publishes reprints of outstanding essays, articles, and lectures.

A non-partisan effort, the Center is supported by contributions from foundations, corporations, and individuals.

Ethics and Public Policy Reprints

1. **Nuclear Energy Politics: Moralism vs. Ethics,** *Margaret N. Maxey*
2. **The World Council of Churches and Radical Chic,** *Richard Neuhaus*
3. **Western Guilt and Third World Poverty,** *P. T. Bauer*
4. **The United States in Opposition,** *Daniel Patrick Moynihan*
5. **Patterns of Black Excellence,** *Thomas Sowell*
6. **Why Arms Control Has Failed,** *Edward N. Luttwak*
7. **Environmentalism and the Leisure Class,** *William Tucker*
8. **A Search for Sanity in Antitrust,** *Walter Guzzardi, Jr.*
9. **Ethics and the New Class,** *Peter L. Berger*
10. **Will Lawyering Strangle Capitalism?** *Laurence H. Silberman*
    The rapid growth of the legal process has reduced the scope for private decision-making and the political process, threatening the vitality of capitalism and democracy.
11. **Is Capital Punishment Just?** *Ernest van den Haag*
    The author concludes that it deters violent crime, affirms social values, and is just.
12. **The Case for Doing Business in South Africa,** *Herman Nickel*
    Most economic and racial group leaders in South Africa insist that reduced U.S. investment would cause unemployment and retard racial justice.
13. **Regulation and the New Class,** *Paul H. Weaver*
    An influential element of the upper-middle class places its confidence in government regulation and profoundly distrusts private enterprise.
14. **Trendier Than Thou: The Episcopal Church and the Secular World,** *Paul Seabury*
    A critique of recent efforts to make the church relevant to current secular causes.
15. **The Press and American Politics**
    J. William Fulbright, Raymond Price, and Irving Kristol
    A politician, a President's speechwriter, and a social philosopher find that the American press is often arrogant and its political reporting is frequently slanted.
16. **Is the New Morality Destroying America?** *Clare Boothe Luce*
    The recent decay of the American family and of society generally can be arrested only by the reaffirmation of a "universal morality."
17. **Politicizing Christianity: Focus on South Africa,** *Edward Norman*
    A critique of the new "liberation theology," which identifies the Christian mission with revolutionary and sometimes terrorist causes.
18. **Alienation and U.S. Foreign Policy,** *Paul Craig Roberts*
    Excessive self-criticism in America and a sense of guilt about our shortcomings erode our capacity to respond effectively to the Soviet military and ideological challenge.
19. **The Cost of America's Retreat,** *Ben J. Wattenberg*
    In the wake of Vietnam, America's power and influence have dangerously receded. We must defend freedom by a posture of "peace through strength."
20. **The Soul of Man Under Socialism,** *Vladimir Bukovsky*
    An exile who spent twelve years in Soviet prisons vividly portrays the impact of a totalitarian system on human dignity and self-respect.
21. **What It Means to Be Number Two**
    Fred Charles Iklé, With a Response by Radomir Bogdanov and Lev Semeiko
    A former top SALT negotiator says American weakness, bordering on inferiority, encourages Soviet expansion. Two Soviet officials dispute his claims.

Reprints are $1 each. Postpaid if payment accompanies order.
Orders of $10 or more, 10 per cent discount.